D1454573

In search of
ALFRED
THE GREAT

In search of

ALFRED THE GREAT

The King
The Grave
The Legend

EDOARDO ALBERT & KATIE TUCKER

AMBERLEY

To Harriet

First published 2014

Amberley Publishing
The Hill, Stroud
Gloucestershire, GL5 4EP

www.amberley-books.com

British Library Cataloguing in Publication Data.
A catalogue record for this book is available from the British Library.

ISBN 978 1 4456 3894 2 (hardback)
ISBN 978 1 4456 3906 2 (ebook)

Typeset in 11.5pt on 13pt Sabon.
Typesetting and Origination by Amberley Publishing.
Printed in the UK.

CONTENTS

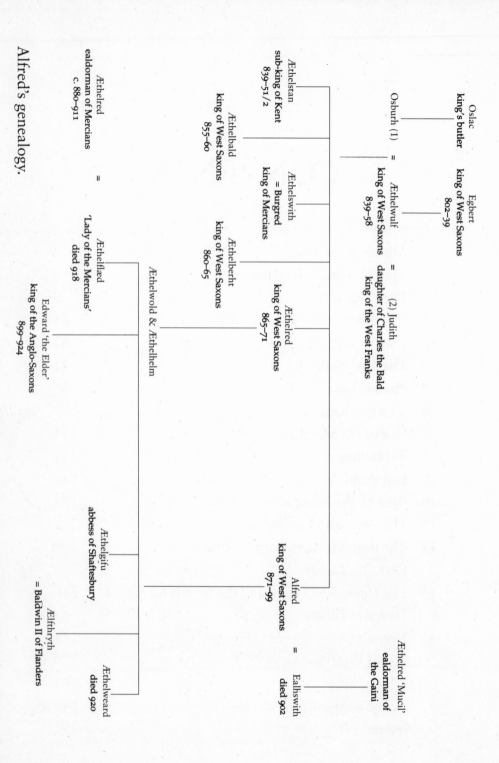

Alfred's genealogy.

1

The King at Bay

The king was a king no more. As he rode west, keeping to tracks through forest and wood, moving at dusk and dawn and laying up during the day, his rule had shrivelled to the men, women and children of his own household. From being king of Wessex, the lord of all the people from beyond the rushing waters of the River Tamar in the west to the rich fields of the Isle of Thanet in the east, he now had so few men at his command that the old laws would call him the leader of a band of brigands, not a king.

Alfred, son of Æthelwulf, king of the West Saxons, ran. Behind him, the takers of his land and kingdom fanned out, searching for the fleeing king and letting the leading men of Wessex know, in no uncertain terms, that they faced a stark choice: come to terms with their new Viking lord, Guthrum, or lose land, livelihood … life. After all, they had already taken three of the four Anglo-Saxon kingdoms. Now, with Alfred on the run, what was to stop them taking the fourth? It's no surprise that, faced with this choice, some of the magnates of Wessex decided to make their peace with the new power in the land.

As he skulked through the frozen land, forced into raiding the winter stores of his own people to sustain himself and his men, Alfred drank a cup of bitterness. For the Viking army had come upon him unannounced and unexpectedly, in the dead of winter when the ground was bare and concealment hardest. For his enemies to have reached all but to the walls of his hall in Chippenham with no warning suggested that they had bought the silence of their passage through his realm. Sitting, wrapped in his cloak, breath misting before a meagre fire, Alfred searched in memory the faces and words of the great men of his realm, seeking intimations of treason. Cuthred, ealdorman of Hampshire, Ælfstan, Dorset's ealdorman, Mucel and Eardwulf; he had known them all since boyhood, he had listened to them debating in council with his father, but where were they now? The few men he could spare he had sent to them, asking for soldiers, for word that they would rally to him. The messengers had returned carrying weasel words or, in some cases, they had not returned at all. Alfred recalled their faces again, the closed eyes and pressed mouths that he had seen at witan, the gathering of the king's councillors, the sign of men with sealed hearts who waited to see which way the witan leaned before adding their weight to the consensus. Now, too, they waited, holding fast to their lands and their wealth, waiting for the storm to pass and the day to bring long sight.

But if they waited, Alfred suspected another must have already decided who would be master of this struggle.

Wulfhere, ealdorman of Wiltshire, the man who governed the shire in the name of the king, the magnate in whose land Alfred had passed the twelve days of Christmas. More to the point, the man who had either so signally failed in his duty that he had not noticed a Viking army marching through his territory, or the man who had already agreed with Guthrum, the Viking leader, to hand over his king to the Danes.

In that, at least, Wulfhere had failed. Warning had reached Alfred, on the twelfth day of Christmas, when gifts were given to commemorate the gifts of the wise men to the infant Messiah, and, faced with the decision to fight, and die, or flee, the king had chosen to run. Now, in the bitter depths of winter, Alfred had to find a hope. The other Anglo-Saxon kingdoms, Northumbria, East Anglia, Mercia, had already fallen to the Great Heathen Army.

The feuding claimants to the throne of Northumbria were defeated in battle against the Vikings, and, later poets attest, one of them, who had incurred the particular enmity of a Viking leader, was put to death through the pagan rite of the blood eagle: sacrificed to Odin by having his chest opened and his lungs spread wide in a grotesque and bloody parody of the wings of an eagle. So the first great kingdom of the Anglo-Saxons had fallen – open warfare had failed as a means of defeating the Vikings.

King Edmund of East Anglia engaged the Great Heathen Army with faith. Taken by surprise when the Vikings – who had previously sworn friendship to him and his people – turned upon him, a later hagiographer relates that he chose to willingly embrace a martyr's death when the pagans gave him an ultimatum: submit or die.

The king of Mercia, Burgred, had chosen a different path. A man, like Edmund, seriously committed to his Christian faith despite being a warrior, Burgred decided to lay down his crown and leave his kingdom rather than lead his people in futile and bloody resistance to the Vikings.

Three kings, three responses to the threat of the Great Heathen Army: resistance, martyrdom, non-resistance. Two of the three kings of the defeated Anglo-Saxon kingdoms had drawn on Christian models for their response, indicating how deeply that faith had penetrated the mind world of, at least, the upper echelons of Anglo-Saxon society. Alfred, on the run in Wessex, was no less committed to his faith than Edmund and Burgred, and as he made hasty, stealthy camps, he must have searched deeply in heart and memory for what he was to do.

The answer also came from his faith, but from the books of the Old Testament, in particular the Psalms, the songs of praise and desolation that form the core of the Church's daily prayer. Many of the Psalms are ascribed to David, to a time when he was a fugitive in the wilderness, being hunted by a king who had turned upon him. Now Alfred too was a fugitive, and as the firelight cast its shadows upon his face, Alfred decided that he would follow the path of David: he would become a wraith in the wilderness, a witness of faithfulness to his people and of defiance to his enemies.

But this was a time when cultures and faiths mixed and clashed. Serious Christian though Alfred was, there was another example he called upon *in extremis*: that of his enemies. Alfred had spent his entire adult life fighting the Vikings. As ætheling, that is a prince of the royal house, he had stood beside his father and his brothers in many battles. More often, he had raised his forces only to arrive too late at a scene of devastation, the raiders having already made off with their loot. Thus Alfred had learned through first-hand, bitter experience the strategic advantage of being a mobile attacker able to raid at a time and place of your own choosing against people tied down by their own defences.

Very well. Guthrum had taken the kingdom from him. Time to see how Guthrum would fare when Alfred went Viking on him.

Now, suddenly, with his kingdom taken from him, Alfred was freed from the obligations of defence and he found he had a huge advantage over his enemies: he knew the land. He and his men had ridden over it, walked across it, hunted through it for all their lives; they knew where to ford rivers, they knew the hidden tracks through forests and the secret ways through marsh. Although Guthrum had taken the royal vills scattered through Wiltshire – roughly twenty miles apart, the distance the peripatetic king and his household could travel in a day – and the winter stores kept within them, he could only enforce his rule by persuading, suborning or intimidating the great men of the kingdom to accept that there was a new power in the land, and to follow it. For, in a time when communication ran no faster than a horse and power was intensely personal, a king could only rule with the co-operation of the people he governed. The ruler sat at the centre of a chain of influence, pulling ropes of loyalty and fear, but he depended on those further along the chains transmitting his commands downwards from the king, through the ealdormen in charge of each shire, to the reeves that supervised ports and local districts. These were the agents of the king's authority, and the means by which Guthrum had to take control of his new kingdom. If Alfred had died in battle, or fled abroad, it would have been a relatively straightforward matter for the Viking to place a pliant noble on the throne of Wessex and, through him, rule. Indeed, it is possible that Wulfhere, ealdorman of Wiltshire, had agreed to be Guthrum's man in return for the title of king. As Alfred ghosted through Wiltshire in the early months of 878, he sent out messengers to the agents of royal authority throughout the surrounding shires, letting them know he was still alive and would remain faithful to his people. The question was, would his people remain faithful to him?

The question was answered, in part, by the reaction of the men of Devon and the shire's ealdorman, Odda, to the arrival of another Viking fleet on their shore during this time of Alfred's eclipse. Alfred, and the few men he had with him, were about to be trapped between Guthrum's patrols, operating from Chippenham, and this new Viking army, led by Ubba, one of the sons of the legendary Ragnar Lothbrok.

As the Vikings disembarked on the beach east of modern-day Lynmouth, they saw Ealdorman Odda and his men waiting for them. As an experienced Viking warlord, it's likely Ubba felt no great trepidation at thus being met. The ealdorman of Devon, with the nervous and inexperienced farmers and peasants that formed most of his army, had decided not to contest the Viking landing, but rather to take a defensive position at the top of Countisbury Hill, an 850-foot-high ridge overlooking the beach, digging further ramparts to make the existing defences better. But the Viking saw that there was no water supply at the top of the hill. Furthermore, his battle standard, the famous raven banner, had flown high in the wind on their crossing from south Wales. The raven was a bird sacred to the Vikings, for Odin, Gallows Lord and All-Father, had, upon his shoulders, two ravens, Thought and Memory, that he sent out each day to bring him news of the world. The raven banner of Ubba had been woven for him by his sisters and, according to widespread belief, it would fly strongly before victory but hang limply before defeat.

Ubba, seeing the raven banner fluttering in the wind blowing in from the sea, ordered his men to besiege the hill. There was no need for anything rash. All they had to do was wait, and time and thirst would drive Odda and the men of Devon from their fort and into the hands of the Vikings.

We do not know how long the siege lasted, but before his men had been weakened by privation, Ealdorman Odda came to the same conclusion as the man besieging him: to wait was to die. So, as dawn was breaking, he led the men of Devon from behind their earthworks and upon the Vikings. The besiegers were taken utterly by surprise and routed. Ubba's tale came to an end beneath an Anglo-Saxon sword, as did the lives of somewhere around a thousand of his fellow Vikings. Even his battle banner, having failed in its foretelling, was captured by the victorious men of Devon. Rather than capitulating before their new Viking lords, the men of Wessex had won a famous victory.

News of Odda's triumph must have reached Alfred as quickly as it reached Guthrum – indeed, in all likelihood, it got to him first – and perhaps it was the catalyst for his decision to make a base for his small guerrilla army.

Athelney, in the Somerset Levels, takes its name from Old English and means 'Isle of Princes'. It's not an island now, or at least, not usually. The record-breaking rain of the winter of 2013/14 saw the Levels flooded, and gave us, watching the news, some inkling of the landscape there before drainage and clearance turned 'a most dismal fen ... now consisting of bogs, now of marshes, sometimes of pools, concealed by black mists, sometimes studded with wooded islands and traversed by the windings of tortuous streams'[1] into farmland. The name suggests that the area was well known to Alfred – perhaps the young æthelings had used it as a base for hunting trips into the marsh wilderness. Here, on this island that floated between land and water, Alfred left history and entered a world of myth. Later, legends accumulated about the king's time on Athelney; here, he sat tending the cakes of a lowly swineherd who had given him shelter, not knowing a king slept in his hut, and, wrapped up in thought, the king did not smell them burning. Nor did he demur at the scolding the swineherd's wife gave him, but accepted it as due pay for the loss of his kingdom. Here, Alfred met, in dream and vision and, perhaps, in the flesh, the saints of England.

And it was from this island redoubt that Alfred slipped forth and, disguised as a minstrel, infiltrated the Viking camp and learned their plans. Since Alfred and Guthrum had already met, and negotiated, face to face, this last story seems the most unlikely of all. But whatever the truth of the stories, a glance at the geography around Athelney shows how well it could serve as Alfred's base. Its one weakness was that it could, conceivably, be reached by Viking ships, poling down the River Tone after sailing inland along the River Parrett. But the death

of Ubba and the defeat of his forces by the men of Devon
– who presumably remained on guard against any further
naval incursions – freed Alfred from the worry of amphibious
assault. Secure on Athelney, Alfred had easy access to a
network of Roman roads and ancient tracks that crisscrossed
Wessex, allowing him the mobility that had always been the
chief strategic advantage of his enemies. While at Athelney,
Alfred was joined by the ealdorman of Somerset, Æthelnoth.
With complete knowledge of the area's geography and links
to all the people with influence in the locality, Æthelnoth
became a key member of Alfred's household as the king sent
out raiding parties, spies and messengers.

Alfred arrived on Athelney around Easter, that is, 23 March
878. He had been a fugitive for nearly three months, through
the harshest part of the winter. Nowadays, there is very little
to see at Athelney. The land has been drained, the stands of
alder cut down, and many years of ploughing and farming
have lowered the former island until it barely stands proud of
the surrounding fields. The railway line to Taunton runs just
south of Athelney, and the monument to King Alfred, raised by
Sir John Slade in 1801, is just visible from the train. Standing
atop Athelney, it comes as a surprise just how small a space
this is: some 360 paces long and 50 paces wide. Not much of a
kingdom for a king. In such a restricted space, Alfred can only
have had room for the smallest of guerrilla armies – maybe a
hundred men or so. But, having driven Alfred and the kingdom
of Wessex to the point of extinction, Guthrum was unable to
finish the job. Just under a mile north-east of Athelney, on the
far bank of the confluence of the rivers Tone and Parrett, is the
steep little mound of Burrow Mump, standing seventy-nine

feet proud of the surrounding flatland; it would have made an ideal watchtower, giving Alfred ample warning of any attempt by Guthrum to infiltrate men towards Athelney. With his base secure, Alfred set about retaking his kingdom. He later wrote,

> In the case of the king, the resources and tools with which to rule are that he have his land fully manned: he must have praying men, fighting men and working men.[2]

The question was, did Alfred have the men to fight for him? Apart from the men of his own household, and those of the faithful Æthelnoth, there were no professional warriors he could call upon. Each shire was responsible for its own defence, raising an army, the fyrd, from the nobility and free men of the shire. Although a man could be fined for failing to answer the call to military service, if the local gentry, the shire reeves and the ealdorman of a county decided not to enforce a call-up there was no way that Alfred could call the men to him. So, where lay the loyalty of the men of Somerset, of Wiltshire, of Hampshire?

During the weeks after Easter, Alfred had sent clandestine messages to the ealdormen and reeves of Somerset, Wiltshire and Hampshire, summoning them and their fyrds to meet him at Egbert's Stone on 4 May 878. The exact location of this stone is much argued about, but it was a well-known meeting point of the time, lying 'in the eastern part of Selwood Forest',[3] an ancient and vast forest that stood on the borders of Somerset, Wiltshire and Hampshire. As Alfred rode from his 'fen-fastness' to this clearing in a remnant of the ancient wildwood, he knew that his future, and the future of his kingdom, rested upon how many would hear his call and come to stake their lives with his. As the new spring green closed over his head and he entered the forest, Alfred must have wandered in memory through the years of his life up until then, and how he had come to this moment of destiny ...

2

The Boy Born
Not to Be King

As Alfred rode beneath the green roof of Selwood Forest along the ancient track, the Hardway, towards Egbert's Stone, he remembered. There was a good chance that he would be dead within days, and his family extinguished, so his thoughts wandered back to his childhood, lingering over the memories most valuable to him. And, uniquely for a king of this era, we have some idea of which memories these were, for Alfred told us.

The Dark Ages are, officially, no longer the Dark Ages but the early medieval period. Historians and archaeologists have, quite rightly, bridled about the connotations of ignorance and stupidity applied to an era when many of the foundations of modern society were laid, from the rule of law and the agrarian revolution to the philosophical presumption of a rational universe. But in one aspect, darkness did fall over part of Europe with the fall of the Roman Empire, and nowhere more so than Britain: history ended. The Romano-

Britons who first invited and then fought incoming bands of Germanic mercenaries and freebooters were literate, Christian and, initially at least, imbued with Romanitas. The incoming Angles, Saxons, Jutes and Frisians, and whoever else came along for the pickings, were illiterate, pagan and too busy carving out kingdoms to be worried about Germanitas. So, for a couple of centuries after AD 410, when the legions officially withdrew from Britain, silence falls. Even when the English emerge, blinking, back into the light of history, ushered back on stage in Bede's people-defining work, the *Ecclesiastical History of the English People* (finished around 731), there is still little documentary evidence of the inward thoughts and memories of kings, and even less for the century after Bede, when Viking incursions brought about a drastic decline in literacy and scholarship.

But with Alfred it is different. We have a short biography of the king, written by Asser, a Welsh bishop who came into the king's service around 885 and remained with Alfred for the rest of his life. It's a curious work, giving the impression of being notes towards a biography rather than a complete work, but it provides much information unobtainable about any other king of the period. Then, and even more extraordinary, we have some of Alfred's own writing, in translations of various classic texts into English and his glosses and introductions to the books. In no other monarch of the period do we have a direct record of his thoughts; Alfred is unique in this, as he is in many other ways.

As a friend and confidant of Alfred, Asser heard at first hand the king's reminiscences of his childhood and recorded them. So, as Alfred rode towards his destiny, it is likely his mind went back to some of the events Asser described. The king of Wessex, the last remaining king of the Anglo-Saxons, was twenty-nine. Facing death, he no doubt did what all young men do in such circumstances: he thought of his mother, Osburh.

Osburh was the daughter of Oslac, who was butler to her husband-to-be, King Æthelwulf. This might sound a rather low status for the future spouse of the king, but the role of butler in Wessex was much more than greeting visitors to the great hall and taking their swords; rather, he was the king's executive. Her father claimed descent from the legendary conquerors of the Isle of Wight, thus making her of royal blood. But despite this nobility, Osburh was not queen, but rather the king's wife, for the house of Wessex did not allow a woman to reign alongside her husband. This was unusual. Anglo-Saxon England allowed a considerable degree of autonomy, freedom and even power to women. In law, a woman's weregild, the compensation price to be paid to relatives if she was killed, was the same as that for a man of equal status. But in some cases women ranked even higher than men, most notably in the case of double monasteries, religious foundations of nuns and monks where the separate communities were united under the rule of a female abbess. Hilda (*c.* 614–680), the abbess of Whitby, was the most widely known of such women, but there were many others, including Etheldreda (Æthelthryth; 636–679), the founder of the Abbey of Ely, and Æthelburh (d. *c.* 688), who founded Barking Abbey. In fact, so unusual was the low status of the wives of the kings of Wessex that Asser sets out to tell his readers how 'this perverse and detestable custom, contrary to the practice of all Germanic peoples'[1] arose. It was all because of a wicked queen called Eadburh.

Asser tells the story at some length, claiming that he had heard it often from Alfred himself. It is meant as a warning tale, but it is hard to read it without feeling considerable admiration for such a remarkable woman. Eadburh (*fl.* 789–802) was the daughter of Offa, the great king of Mercia and a man sufficiently powerful that he could cause a massive, and massively long, earthwork to be dug separating his kingdom from the hostile kingdom of Powys – Offa's Dyke. As part of the power politics of the eighth century, Offa married his daughter to Beorhtric (d. 802), king of Wessex; the price was alliance between the two kingdoms, with Mercia definitely the senior partner. And, according to Asser, Eadburh set out to make sure that everybody knew exactly who was in charge. Once she had charmed the king – no small matter in a day when royal marriages were entirely practical exercises in power – she set about undermining everyone else who had Beorhtric's favour, through lies and trickery. But if the dark arts of spin proved insufficient to bring a rival down, Eadburh turned to the favoured tool of the courtly schemer: poison. When her husband would not accept her calumnies against a particular favourite, Ealdorman Worr, the queen attempted to poison him but Beorhtric also drank from the fatal cup, and both men died.

The indefatigable queen was not about to let the little matter of a dead husband get in her way so, taking as much of the wealth of Wessex with her as could be transported, she set off for the court of Emperor Charlemagne, the king of the Franks and the most powerful man in Europe. Much of the wealth of an Anglo-Saxon kingdom was portable. Eadburh arrived at Charlemagne's court with enough gold to buy a king, and the political contacts to match. Charlemagne asked her to choose between him and his son. Here, unfortunately, Eadburh made a fatal error. Judging, no doubt correctly, that Charlemagne, by that time well into his fifties, would be a harder man to influence than any of his sons, she said, 'If the choice is left to me, I choose your son, as he is younger than you.'[2]

To which, Asser reports, Charlemagne replied, 'Had you chosen me, you would have had my son; but because you have chosen my son, you will have neither him nor me.'[3]

As consolation, Charlemagne gave Eadburh the rule of a large convent. This was a powerful and far from unpleasant appointment, and a frequently employed solution for what to do with princesses and queens whose husbands had died. Eadburh took to it with gusto – somewhat too much gusto, as she was apparently caught in flagrante delicto with a visitor from England and, on Charlemagne's orders, ejected from the convent, eventually ending her life, with just a single servant for company, at Pavia, a town in Lombardy that lay on the pilgrim road to Rome.

There's no independent evidence for Eadburh's career as poisoner and debaucher, although as daughter of Offa, and conscious of her father as far the more powerful partner in the alliance with Wessex, she would no doubt have been an imperious figure. But it is worth bearing in mind that one of the stipulations for her marriage to Beorhtric was the expulsion of a powerful noble, Ecgberht. According to the terse record in the *Anglo-Saxon Chronicle*, the year 802 saw the deaths of Beorhtric and Ealdorman Worr, and the accession of Ecgberht to the throne of Wessex. It may be that Beorhtric and Worr, rather than dying from poison, died under the sword of Ecgberht and his men, and the queen, gathering whatever gold she could, immediately fled. To fortify his claims to the throne, it would have made sense for Ecgberht to blacken Eadburh's name. However, there is no record of any children from the marriage of Beorhtric and Eadburh, thus reducing her danger to Ecgberht and his successors. Whatever the truth of how Ecgberht came to the throne, he would prove the fount of English kingship; for he was grandfather to Alfred the Great and, ultimately, the British royal family.

According to Asser, since the infamous reign of Queen Eadburh the West Saxons had resolved that they would never allow a king to reign over them who put a queen beside him on the throne – his wife had to remain quietly in the background, accorded the title 'king's wife' but nothing more. Alfred's mother, Osburh, fulfilled this role perfectly and, as such, makes barely a mark on the historical record. But her son remembered her with love.

Born around 849 (at the earliest 848, the latest 850), Alfred was the youngest of Osburh's five sons and one daughter, born late and out of time and, as a result, almost certainly the pet of the family. Asser tells us that, most unusually, Alfred was raised entirely by his own parents, rather than being fostered out to a relative for part of his childhood, as was the custom among the nobility of the time. Such a practice cemented the personal relationships and obligations that were the glue binding society together, but Alfred stayed with his mother and father. Alfred's eldest brother, Æthelstan, was possibly as much as twenty years older than him, and there were wide gaps between him and most of his siblings; only Æthelred, the last before Alfred, was anywhere near him in age. The older brothers, Æthelstan, Æthelbald, Æthelberht and Æthelred, and Æthelswith, his sister, all bore names that began with the prefix Æthel, which means 'noble'; it was common practice, in a time before surnames, to indicate family relationship by using the same prefix for siblings. Ælfræd, as Alfred's name would have been spelled, however, was different; the prefix means 'elf' and the suffix 'counsel' or 'wisdom' – there is no clue in the historical record as to why his father and mother chose to break their own precedent with their final, and unexpected, son.

Apart from her lineage and the fact that she was 'a most religious woman, noble in character',[4] only one other incident casts any light on Osburh's character, but it is a revealing light, both about her and her youngest son.

One day, the story goes, Osburh showed her sons a book of poetry, written in English. 'I shall give this book to whichever one of you can learn it the fastest,' she said.[5] Alfred, entranced by the beauty of the initial letter – think on the work lavished on the first letter of each chapter of the Lindisfarne Gospels for an, admittedly lofty, comparison – asked, 'Will you really give this book to the one of us who can understand it the soonest and recite it to you?' Osburh, smiling at her enthusiastic youngest son, confirmed she would, whereupon Alfred rushed off with it to his tutor – the boy could not read himself yet – and had the book recited to him until he had learned the songs off by heart, a feat no doubt facilitated by the intrinsic mnemonic quality of a poetry that was meant to be memorised and recited. The poems learned, Alfred recited the book back to his mother, and received his prize.

The memory was significant enough to Alfred for him to tell it to Asser, some thirty years after Osburh's death. But it also tells us that Osburh could, almost certainly, read herself, and that she played a major part in the education of her children. She may not have been a queen, but she played a key part in the formation of her son.

The world into which Alfred was born was changing. The eighth century had been something of a golden age of Anglo-Saxon scholarship and culture, to such an extent that a monk, Bede, who never ventured more than a day's journey from Jarrow could be the foremost scholar in Europe, and the most powerful king of the time, Charlemagne, poached scholars from York to kick-start his programme of ecclesiastical renewal. The myriad petty kingdoms that had characterised Britain in the sixth and seventh centuries had gradually consolidated, by sword or alliance, leaving four major Anglo-Saxon realms: Northumbria, Mercia, East Anglia and Wessex; although the remaining kingdoms of the Britons remained fragmented and prone to internecine warfare, the catastrophic defeat suffered by the Northumbrians at the Battle of Nechtansmere in 685 ensured that the north, the Scotland of the future, remained under the control of the Picts and the men of Dal Riata.

But, in one of the most famous passages in the *Anglo-Saxon Chronicle*, the eighth century ended with the sacking of the monastery at Lindisfarne.

A.D. 793. This year came dreadful fore-warnings over the land of the Northumbrians, terrifying the people most woefully:

these were immense sheets of light rushing through the air, and whirlwinds, and fiery dragons flying across the firmament. These tremendous tokens were soon followed by a great famine: and not long after, on the sixth day before the ides of January in the same year, the harrowing inroads of heathen men made lamentable havoc in the church of God in Holy-island, by rapine and slaughter.[6]

The Vikings had come.

By the time Alfred was born, the initial raids, undertaken by small numbers of men taking advantage of the unpreparedness of the peoples of north-eastern Europe, had transformed into mobile amphibious armies, professional and acutely sensitive to the shifting political strength of the kings they raided and accommodated. The death of Charlemagne in 814 had removed the towering presence of the first Holy Roman Emperor from the European stage, and the civil wars between his sons and grandsons that followed through the rest of the ninth century allowed enterprising Viking armies to play off the contending kings against each other, as well as providing the opportunity to plunder the disputed territories between the heartlands of each claimant. It was the perfect situation for an enterprising Viking chief, and the ruthlessly Hobbesian world they inhabited served to bring to the top the most ruthless and the most venturesome. And the great thing was, if the situation grew too hazardous in one place, they could always go somewhere else. Despite their modern reputation as berserk warriors, the Vikings avoided battle wherever they could; far better to fall upon lightly defended monasteries and halls rather than face men fighting for their families and their livelihoods. As professional warriors, they were all too aware of the possibility of catastrophe in any battle; far better to stack the odds in their favour. One of the best ways of doing that was to demand protection money: a promise to leave, and to leave the kingdom unharmed, on the payment of sufficient money. Such was the effectiveness of the various Viking armies that this ploy worked more often than not; what made it even sweeter was the opportunity it offered to return, a year or two later, and demand more money. The Vikings had succeeded in turning the warring kingdoms of Europe into milch cows, and they squeezed hard.

So, with Viking flotillas patrolling the navigable rivers of Francia and his own kingdom having survived a major attack in 851, it might seem surprising that King Æthelwulf would choose to dispatch his youngest son, and possibly Æthelred, Alfred's older brother, on pilgrimage to Rome. Alfred was only four, Æthelred a few years older, and the journey was long, arduous and dangerous.

Even today, such a journey would remain locked in memory. For Alfred, it must have been one of the most formative experiences of his life. Æthelwulf had prepared the way as much as possible for his sons, sending letters to the kings of the kingdoms they would pass through, requesting safe passage and assistance for the young æthelings. Æthelwulf was an intensely devout man. He had fought the Vikings twice, in 843, when the *Chronicle* records he fought at Charmouth against a raiding party from thirty-five ships, and lost, and again in 851, when the situation was rapidly worsening, as, for the first time, the Vikings had overwintered in England, making a fortified camp on the Isle of Thanet and continuing with their depredations during the next campaigning season. This time, Æthelwulf and his second son, Æthelbald, met the Viking army and 'with the West Saxon levies fought against them at *Acleah* and there made the greatest slaughter of a heathen host that we have heard tell of up to this present day'.[7] But the pressure was increasing, and Æthelwulf needed help, divine help. He had already lost his eldest son, whether from war or natural causes we do not know, and although Æthelbald was proving an excellent commander, the king must have given thanks that God had provided him with so many sons.

Warfare, in the early medieval period, was very different from the practices of the high medieval and later eras, when kings and generals generally conducted battles from a place of vantage and safety. Even if disaster should befall in battle and they be defeated, kings and nobles were too valuable to be killed even if they should be captured – there's a reason for the phrase 'a king's ransom' meaning a vast amount of money. But in the early medieval period there was no hiding place, even for the rich and powerful. Æthelwulf, and his sons and ealdormen, had to take the leading place in the battle line, at the centre of the shield wall. Battle, in the end, came down to two exhausted lines of men, face to face and body to body, shoving, striking, pushing and kicking until a breach opened in one or other of the shield walls and, the dam broken, the static scrum of men turned into a melee, with one side fleeing, leaving the victors, as the sources graphically report, in possession of 'the field of slaughter'. It was brutal, grinding labour and though the king would be surrounded by his best men, men trained for warfare all their lives and tough in a way beyond our understanding today, in the end the quickest and most decisive way to end a battle was to kill the opposing leader. A king, in battle, was the ultimate target as well as the chief rallying point – let him fall, and then the battle was surely lost. For Vikings, intent on plunder, there was additional incentive for killing the king – stripping the corpse. A king, an ealdorman, any noble, was tricked out to match his status, with weapons and armour that were emblems of wealth as much as engines of death. The early medieval equivalent to winning the lottery was to be left standing on the battlefield with limbs intact and sufficient energy to strip the corpses of the dead.

Æthelwulf knew all too well that to be a king at this time was no recipe for long life. But he would fight for his sons in every way he could, in this life and in the next, for the first was preparation and qualification for the latter. He could not spare Æthelbald, nor Æthelberht, the next oldest. They were grown now, old enough to stand in the shield wall and to act as witnesses to royal charters, signing their names above those of the local magnates. But although Alfred and Æthelred were too young for war, they were old enough for diplomacy, and for intercession.

Bede, in the *Ecclesiastical History*, relates the famous story of what prompted Pope Gregory the Great to dispatch missionaries to the pagan Anglo-Saxons.

I must here relate a story, handed down to us by the tradition of our forebears, which explains Gregory's deep desire for the salvation of our nation. We are told that one day some merchants who had recently arrived in Rome displayed their many wares in the market-place. Among the crowd who thronged to buy was Gregory, who saw among other merchandise some boys exposed for sale. These had fair complexions, fine-cut features and beautiful hair. Looking at them with interest, he enquired from what country and what part of the world they came. 'They come from the island of Britain,' he was told, 'where all the people have this appearance.' He then asked whether the islanders were Christians, or whether they were still ignorant heathens. 'They are pagans,' he was informed. 'Alas!' said Gregory with a heartfelt sigh: 'how sad that such bright-faced folk are still in the grasp of the author of darkness, and that such graceful features conceal minds devoid of God's grace! What is the name of this race?' 'They are called Angles,' he was told. 'That is appropriate,' he said, 'for they have angelic faces, and it is right that they should become joint-heirs with the angels in heaven. And what is the name of the province from which they have been brought?' 'Deira,' was the answer. 'Good. They shall indeed be rescued *de ira* – from wrath – and called to the mercy of Christ. And what is the name of their king?' 'Aelle,' he was told. 'Then,' said Gregory, making play on the name, 'it is right that their land should echo the praise of God our Creator in the word *Alleluia*.'[8]

This story, whether true or not, resonated among the Anglo-Saxons, creating a special reverence for the See of Peter and a determination, among many of them, to visit Rome as pilgrims, so much so that there was a Schola Saxonum (Saxon School) in the city, in Borgo, which lies between the Castel Sant Angelo and the Vatican. In fact, the name 'Borgo' is an Italianised version of 'burh', the Old English word for a fortified dwelling place – it had to be fortified as even Rome was subject to pirate attacks, although in its case the raiders were Saracens rather than Vikings. (However, in one truly magnificent case of mistaken identity, a Viking chieftain named Hæsten led marauders around Spain and through the Straits of Gibraltar, raiding Christian and Islamic kingdoms as he went, aiming for the Eternal City itself. Ambition, and the desire for glory, was never lacking in Viking chieftains and Hæsten had already razed Paris to the ground, so Rome must have seemed the only way of topping that achievement. However, according to the chronicler Dudo of Saint-Quentin, Hæsten mistook the city of Luna, some two hundred miles north of Rome, for the city itself and, after pretending to be a dying penitent seeking baptism, Hæsten tricked his way into the city and sacked the place. Alfred would one day face Hæsten himself.)

The Schola Saxonum would have provided a particular welcome to the young West Saxon æthelings, for it was founded by a previous king of Wessex, Ine (died *c.* 726), who, after reigning for roughly thirty-five years (an age for the time), abdicated his throne and went as a pilgrim to Rome, where he finally died, having provided a hostelry for the many visitors from his native land.

The Anglo-Saxons had come to see themselves, in part through the prism provided by Bede, as a chosen people, analogous to God's original chosen people. So, when trying to understand the extraordinary dislocation caused by the Viking irruption, they naturally looked to the history of the Jews for a key to understanding. The answer was clear and precise: when the Jews strayed from their covenant with God, when they abandoned his worship and forfeited his practices, tribulation came upon them until they corrected their errors, and God's correction took the all-too-human form of invading armies:

Egyptians, Assyrians, Babylonians. Trying to understand the 'whirlwind that came out of the north' (Ezekiel 1:4), Alfred would later definitively ascribe the action of the Vikings to the winnowing fan of God, scourging a people that had fallen away from him. The four-year-old Alfred would have had no such thoughts, but it is possible that his father did. To earn back God's favour, Æthelwulf dispatched his sons to God's ealdorman on earth, laden with gifts.

Pope Leo IV met the young æthelings in style. Although Rome was a shadow of its former glory, yet it was still a city like nothing Alfred had ever seen before, its buildings, made of the stuff of the living earth, reaching higher than the tallest trees. The princes were used to meeting kings, but nothing and no one they had met before would have prepared them for Leo. Arrayed in the panoply of the pontiff in a building, the old St Peter's Basilica, that was bigger and more magnificent than any town in their kingdom, the pope was a man of extraordinary energy, who had raised the walls of what is still called the Leonine City to protect the parts of Rome east of the Tiber, where the Vatican and Borgo were, from Saracen attacks. We have Alfred's own recollection, relayed through Asser, for the impression Leo left on the four-year-old prince who stood before him.

> He [Pope Leo] anointed the child Alfred as king, ordaining him properly, received him as an adoptive son and confirmed him.[9]

Only, he didn't. That is, the pope did not anoint Alfred king. After all, his older brother was standing beside him, and there were two more, older, æthelings back in Wessex. The royal servants and nobles who had accompanied the young princes were not going to supplant the choice of Æthelwulf, nor the role of the witan, the assembly of the magnates of Wessex, and choose a king when they were 900 miles away from home. But the account Alfred gives us shows how dazzled he was, for we have the pope's own words, in a letter to Æthelwulf, of what he had done when he met the young Alfred:

> We have now graciously received your son Alfred, whom you were anxious to send at this time to the threshold of the Holy Apostles, and we have decorated him, as a spiritual son, with the dignity of the belt [*or* sword] and the vestments of the consulate, as is customary with Roman consuls, because he gave himself into our hands.[10]

It's not hard to see how a four-year-old boy could understand being girded with a belt and sword, and being given the robes of a consul – a purely honorary title by then – as an investiture. Repeating the story many years later to men who saw Alfred as the divinely appointed king who had saved the realm from the Vikings by force and by prayer, it would have been easy to read history forwards and turn a ceremonial into a prophetic anointing, hallowed by the presence of the relics of St Peter himself beneath the altar of the basilica, in the same way that David, the youngest of the sons of Jesse, was anointed king by the prophet Samuel.

But if it was unusual to visit Rome once, Alfred was to do so again, and in short order too. The young æthelings returned to Wessex soon after being presented to Leo, and were back home by spring 854. While they were away, their sister, Æthelswith, had married the king of Mercia, Burgred, cementing the alliance between the two kingdoms. With his relationship to his neighbour secure, Æthelwulf was in a position to make a momentous decision: he too would go as a pilgrim to Rome. Learning from his sons the details of their journey and the welcome they had received must have aided the king in his decision, but there was another factor in play too. Æthelwulf was a widower. We do not know exactly when Osburh died, but the contacts made and strengthened by the journey of the two princes through the land of the Franks had raised a new possibility for Æthelwulf: he could take a Frankish princess as wife.

But before leaving the king had to secure his kingdom. Æthelwulf did that in the way all Anglo-Saxon kings shored up their rule: by giving. In fact, Æthelwulf gave away 10 per cent of his land to the Church and to his magnates; in effect, the king was attempting to buy their loyalty. But it was a hallowed system of mutual exchange: one of the key epithets of a king in Anglo-Saxon poetry was 'ring giver'; the distribution of treasure to his followers by an open-handed ruler was a measure of prestige, esteem and mutual obligation. By giving so much land away – it was called Æthelwulf's 'Decimation' – the king ensured prayers from his lords spiritual and patience from his lords temporal, or so he hoped. With the kingdom secured against his magnates, that left only his sons. Over-eager æthelings, unwilling to wait for incumbent rulers to die, were a perennial source of instability in the Anglo-Saxon kingdoms, particularly since the kingdoms did not have clearly defined laws of succession. With the crown open to whoever could command the support of the witan, it was no surprise that an ætheling might try to assert his right to rule prematurely. Although Æthelred, the brother nearest in age to Alfred, was still too young to aspire to the throne, the same was not true of the two older surviving princes. Working on the principle of dividing and ruling, while he was away Æthelwulf arranged for Æthelbald and Æthelberht, the oldest of the brothers, to split the rule of Wessex between them, with the older, Æthelbald, taking command of the Wessex heartland, and his younger brother, Æthelberht, responsible for the eastern shires of Sussex, Surrey, Kent and Essex.

With the realm divided and as secure as Æthelwulf could make it, the king and a large royal party, with a still very young Prince Alfred among them, left for Rome in the spring of 855. But when they arrived in Rome, they found Alfred's spiritual godfather dead; Leo IV died on 17 July 855. The gifts Æthelwulf had brought were to be laid at the feet of his successor, Benedict III. And rich gifts they were indeed. The *Liber Pontificalis* records the king's largesse: a four-pound crown of pure gold, a gilded silver candle holder, a golden goblet, a robe of imperial purple embossed with golden keys and other religious robes. Æthelwulf also gave generously to the clergy and laity of the city. Although far from the traditional ambit of an Anglo-Saxon king, he was still careful to be the generous 'ring giver', earning the blessing of heaven and the prayers of God's ealdorman on earth.

In contrast to his first visit to Rome, this time Alfred stayed for a whole year. Arriving in the summer shortly after Leo's death, the king and his son had to wait for the election of the pope's successor. This proved a fraught operation, with Emperor Lothar, Charlemagne's grandson and ruler of a thick slice of Europe running from the Low Countries through to northern Italy, attempting to put his own man, Anastasius, into the office. Rome dissolved into faction fights between supporters of Benedict, the already elected pope, and Anastasius, newly installed on the back of the emperor's troops. In the end, a new election was called, which Benedict won overwhelmingly. Surprisingly, the fact that Lothar died on the same day as Benedict was consecrated pope – 29 September 855 – was not seen as a divine judgement on Lothar's attempt to meddle in ecclesiastical affairs.

With a new pope installed, Æthelwulf and Alfred were able to present him with their gifts and settle down to some serious sightseeing. In their case, this must have involved a round of church visiting. As testament to the frequency of Anglo-Saxon pilgrims to Rome, a visitor from Malmesbury in the eighth century compiled an itinerary of forty churches the Anglo-Saxon pilgrim to Rome really should visit. In most cases, the notability of a church depended upon its relics. At first glance, the interest and devotion shown by ninth-century Anglo-Saxons to bones and remains might seem unimaginably distant from us today, but even in 2009, over 100,000 modern-day Britons visited the mortal remains of a nun who died in obscurity over a century before: Thérèse of Lisieux. The desire to be close to the tangible remains of someone holy is strong, and Rome was stuffed full of churches that contained the physical remains of people who were not just saints but, in the case of saints Peter and Paul, apostles, figures – and major figures at that – in the Bible. Being in the presence of their remains was to be, spiritually and imaginatively, transported into the presence of Jesus as he walked the dusty tracks of

Galilee and made his fateful way to Jerusalem. What's more, many relics had miraculous properties, effecting cures and working wonders. Relics made faith physical and tangible, they could be touched, smelled, seen with the eye of the head rather than the eye of the heart.

This year in Rome with his father, visiting God's ealdorman and living in the presence of the apostles, must have sealed the young Alfred's faith. It never seems to have wavered afterwards, despite the desperate straits he and his kingdom were reduced to. Indeed, if we are looking to find the source of the moral and spiritual courage that allowed Alfred to endure the testing that was to come, some of it must have been laid here, during this precious year in his father's company; a young boy made more vulnerable by the recent death of his mother but as a result more open and more aware.

The city they saw was, in terms of population, a pale shadow of its imperial heyday. The emperors had held sway, often shakily, over a city of a million people, but the intervening centuries had seen the populace melt away until, in the ninth century, only 30,000 were left. But the largest town back home, Mercian London, had barely a thousand inhabitants and the biggest town in Wessex, Hamwic (Southampton), would have fitted inside the Baths of Caracalla. Rome, even in decline, dazzled.

But, as Alfred was already only too well aware, all things in this world must pass, and in 856 father and son headed back over the Alps. On the way, they naturally stopped to see the king of the lands they were travelling through, Charles the Bald, another grandson of Charlemagne and the ruler of the western portion of Charlemagne's old empire, the lands that would become France. But it was not just a courtesy visit. Æthelwulf was a widower and Charles had a daughter, Judith, who was now just about of marriageable age. She was twelve. For Æthelwulf, marrying the daughter of the king of the Franks was a great coup, made all the sweeter by the fact that Offa, king of Mercia and the man who had engineered the exile of his father, had petitioned Charlemagne to marry one of the emperor's daughters, only for the outraged Charlemagne to call a trade embargo against the products of Mercia for such effrontery. Now Æthelwulf would succeed where Offa had failed. But marriage came at a price, of course, and the first payment was to acknowledge Judith as queen. No daughter of the king of the Franks could merely be styled as the 'king's wife'; she must, necessarily, be queen in her own right. This, of course, cut straight across the West Saxon tradition that the wife of the king should remain safely in the background – but since the tradition had only started with his father, Æthelwulf decided that, for the sake of such a prestigious marriage, he could dispense with tradition.

Such a union between Anglo-Saxon and European royal houses was very rare. Judith was also Charles's firstborn, although by the time Judith married Æthelwulf, Charles's queen had borne him seven more children, six of whom were still alive, so the union was a major political and dynastic statement. But, at this distance, it is hard to see the advantage the union accrued to Charles. Given the difficulties of long-distance co-ordination, there was little prospect of a military alliance against the Viking threat. In fact, the general pattern of Viking attacks suggested that when one kingdom learned better how to resist their depredations, they would turn to its neighbours, thus giving the European kingdoms a vested interest in the weakness of the lands closest to them. Whatever Charles's motivation, the marriage went ahead, and then, the union made, the young Judith was consecrated queen as well. The West Saxons once again had a queen. Æthelwulf, as he looked at the girl standing beside him, must have hoped Judith would not prove as volatile as Eadburh. Alfred, too, must have found the new arrangements confusing, for his father's new wife was only a few years older than he was, with enough childhood left in her to be playmate as well as stepmother.

The marriage made and the queen crowned, it was time to return home. But it was late in the season, October, when autumnal storms can make a Channel crossing a risky business. But word had reached Æthelwulf to tell him that he could not afford to wait until the calm winds of spring. His eldest son, Æthelbald, whom he had left in charge of the western half of his kingdom, had assumed the crown and, supported by some of the leading magnates of the kingdom, had no intention of relinquishing it to his returning father.

The length of time Æthelwulf had spent abroad suggests that he was confident that the gifts – the 'Decimation' – he had given before leaving were more than sufficient to ensure loyalty from his magnates. What he appears not to have considered is disloyalty from a son. But with the support of the ealdorman of Somerset and the bishop of Sherborne, Æthelbald had taken command from his father. The ealdorman and the bishop were old and trusted companions of Æthelwulf, men he had most probably left as mentors to his son, little dreaming that they would conspire against him. So, when Æthelwulf landed in Kent, in the half of his kingdom he had given to Æthelberht to rule, he had a number of possible choices. He could call on the loyalty of the magnates of the eastern counties and fight to reclaim all his lands. He could, as Anglo-Saxon kings had done before him, retire from the fray and renounce his crown for the penitent pilgrim's life, maybe returning to Rome. Or he could attempt to win the magnates of Wessex back to his side and regain the crown through words rather than blood. Æthelwulf appears to have chosen this latter course. A great council, a witan, of the leading magnates of Wessex was called and Æthelwulf attempted to win his crown back.

He failed. The witan left Æthelbald in charge of the western counties of Wessex, those that he had been given when his father left on his pilgrimage to Rome. As a sop, and a testimony to the dutifulness of his second-eldest son, Æthelberht, Æthelwulf took back control of the eastern shires of his realm but, as Asser admits, 'the western part of the Saxon land has always been more important than the eastern'.[11]

Why did some of Æthelwulf's most trusted lieutenants, not to mention his son, turn against him? For Æthelbald, the key factor may have been his father's new wife. Any son produced by Judith would have the backing – financial, political and possibly even military – of the Carolingian power across the Channel. Thus, it made sense for Æthelbald to secure his rule before such a threat could arise. As for the magnates who supported him, they may have come to the coldly practical conclusion that in the dangerous world in which they lived, they could not afford to support any longer a king who was in his fifties.

It must have been a disorientating return home for Alfred,

and his young stepmother found herself in charge of a much smaller realm than she had anticipated. We may perhaps judge what Alfred made of his brother's conduct by the way, many years later, he translated a classic Latin text into English:

> Very pleasant is it for a man to have wife and children, and yet many children are begotten to their parents' destruction, for many a woman dies in childbirth before she can bear the child; and moreover we have learned that long ago there happened a most unwonted and unnatural evil, to wit that sons conspired together and plotted against their father. Nay, worse still, we have heard in old story how of yore a certain son slew his father; I know not in what way, but we know that it was an inhuman deed.[12]

Æthelwulf was already an old man by the standards of the time when he returned to Wessex and faced his son's rebellion. He had outlasted most of his contemporaries and now, in his fifties, he gave thought to his inheritance, writing his last will and testament. In that, he gave the eastern shires of Wessex to his loyal son, Æthelberht, while, bowing to the facts on the ground, he gave title of the western shires to Æthelbald. Thus, the kingdom was to be divided after Æthelwulf's death between his two eldest surviving sons. But the old king had not forgotten his younger two boys. He bequeathed his personal lands and property in the western shires to Æthelbald, Æthelred and Alfred, with the provision, attested in Alfred's own will, that 'whichever of us should live longest was to succeed to everything'.[13] Thus the old king sought to ensure support for his younger sons after his death. But the old king did not only trouble himself with dynastic concerns. Perhaps the truest, and certainly one of the final, marks of the man was his continuing concern for his people, even after his death:

> [H]e enjoined on his successors after him, right up to the final Day of Judgement, that for every ten hides throughout all his hereditary land one poor man (whether native or foreigner) should be sustained with food, drink and clothing.[14]

For the salvation for his soul, and in gratitude for the treatment he had received in Rome, Æthelwulf further enjoined that every year 9,000 pennies were to be sent to the Eternal City, one-third for the lamps in St Peter's, one-third for the lamps in St Paul's and one-third for use at the discretion of the pope. Although his pilgrimage to Rome cost Æthelwulf dearly in terms of power, he never doubted its efficacy for his soul and his kingdom.

In 858, Æthelwulf died. Alfred, nine years old, stood beside his stepmother, herself only fifteen, as the old king was laid to rest at his estate in Steyning, Sussex. Now, they would both depend on Alfred's brothers.

3

The Invaders Invaded

With her husband, King Æthelwulf, dead, the fifteen-year-old Queen Judith had an obvious path in front of her: she could return to the court of her father, Charles the Bald, going back to the people, the language and the culture she knew. But, displaying the independence of spirit that would mark out the rest of her life, Judith did no such thing. In Wessex she was a queen, indelibly marked as one by the anointing with oil that, at her consecration, changed fundamentally her status as a human being. Judith wanted to remain a queen, in action as well as in status. There was one way of doing so while retaining her independence of action, so she took it. She married the new king of Wessex, Æthelbald, her late husband's son and betrayer, and her stepson.

The decision outraged Alfred's biographer, Asser, and presumably Alfred as well.

Once King Æthelwulf was dead, Æthelbald, his son, against God's prohibition and Christian dignity, and also contrary to the practice of all pagans, took over his father's marriage-bed and married Judith, daughter of Charles [the Bald], king of the Franks.[1]

It was not a decision likely to find favour with a monk, nor with a ten-year-old boy. It was clear, though, why Æthelbald thought the censure the match would attract worth risking, for apart from the wealth Judith brought with her, and the political connections to her father and the Carolingian court, a dowager queen embodied her late husband's realm – marrying Judith strengthened Æthelbald's own claim to the crown.

Although Asser makes clear the dismay with which Alfred greeted the news that his stepmother was to marry his brother, there was nothing the boy could do about it. For the next few years the historical record falls silent, but the likelihood is that Alfred, and Æthelred, went with Judith to the court of their older brother.

Æthelbald's reign was short, however. He died, for reasons not relayed to us, in 860, after a two-year reign. Judith, now sixteen, was a widow again.

Possibly deciding that marrying another of Æthelwulf's sons would be a step too far even for her, Judith chose to return to her father's court. Neither marriage had produced any children, so she was free of the entanglements and opportunities a son would have entailed. 'Selling up the possessions she had acquired',[2] Judith went back to her father and his palace at Senlis. Charles afforded his daughter 'all the honour due to a queen'[3] while he cast around for a suitable replacement husband. Judith, however, proved unwilling to wait; early in

862 she eloped with Baldwin, count of Flanders, and, with the consent of her brother, Louis the Stammerer, married him. Charles the Bald was furious. He petitioned the pope for their excommunication, and they were cast from the Church, but this resourceful couple marshalled diplomatic support and had the excommunication lifted. In the end, Charles bowed to the stubborn will of his remarkable daughter and accepted Baldwin as his son-in-law. Judith had two sons by Baldwin and, bringing the story almost full circle, many years later, one of her boys married Alfred's daughter, Ælfthryth.

In Wessex, Æthelbald's death created a dilemma. Under the terms of Æthelwulf's will, the western shires of Wessex that Æthelbald had controlled during his short reign should now pass to Alfred's older brother Æthelred. Although we don't know exactly how much older than Alfred Æthelred was, he must have still been young, for Alfred himself was only about eleven and there seems to have been a fairly short gap between the two boys. With the threat from the Vikings increasing, the kingdom could not afford a boy king, so Æthelberht moved to unite the eastern shires he ruled with the western counties that had been under the control of his older brother. Wessex was reunited under one ruler. Crucially, this reunification was made with the full agreement of all three surviving brothers. It was so important an agreement that, many years later, Alfred begins his own will by returning to the negotiations of his childhood:

> But it happened that Æthelbald died; and Æthelred and I, with the witness of all the councillors of the West Saxons, entrusted our share to our kinsman King Æthelberht, on condition that

he would restore it to us as much under our control as it was when we entrusted it to him.[4]

In effect, Æthelberht had made his brothers his heirs, and heirs to the whole kingdom, rather than splitting it between them. Whoever lived – and bitter experience had already taught them not to expect longevity – would have sole rule of all the lands from Cornwall to Kent. In a mark of the sincerity of his pledge, in a surviving charter Æthelberht gifted land to a Kentish monastery on the basis of a pledge of loyalty to him *and* his brothers.

In keeping with the new unity that Æthelberht was trying to impart to his kingdom, he brought together in council and at court the magnates of the western and the eastern halves of the land of the West Saxons, and throughout his reign the witness lists of charters shows a far greater degree of union between western and eastern shires than had occurred before. Æthelberht was creating a new kingdom but it was to be his younger brothers who had to defend it from the full weight of the Viking assault, for Æthelberht died in 865, and the kingdom in its entirety passed to Æthelred. Three of the five sons of Æthelwulf were dead, none having reached the age of thirty. Now it was Æthelred's turn to rule and Alfred was at his side, a young man of sixteen himself now.

But first, as when Æthelberht came to the throne, the two remaining brothers made to settle clearly the matter of inheritance, so that there could be clarity of command among the dangers they faced.

Then it so happened that Æthelred succeeded to the kingdom ... [a]nd each of us gave to the other his pledge, that whichever of us lived longer should succeed both to the lands and to the treasures and to all the other's possessions except that part which each of us had bequeathed to his children.[5]

The brothers had effectively agreed that whoever lived would be king of all.

Æthelberht's reign began and ended with Viking raids, but the changing nature of those raids showed clearly the new dangers that were about to engulf Æthelred, Alfred and the other Anglo-Saxon kingdoms in the land.

In 860, when Æthelberht assumed the crown, Viking sea raiders landed on the south coast and, making their way inland, sacked Winchester and ravaged the land around. Then, laden with plunder, they made their way back to their boats. But, weighed down as they were, the Vikings lost the speed of movement that was the crucial element of their strategic success, allowing the ealdormen of Dorset and Hampshire to gather their forces and intercept them. The *Anglo-Saxon Chronicle* tersely reports that they 'fought against the enemy, and putting them to flight, made themselves masters of the field of battle'.[6] Asser puts a more triumphal gloss on the victory: 'The Vikings were cut down everywhere and, when they could resist no longer, they took to flight like women, and the Christians were the masters of the battlefield.'[7]

But in 865, the year Æthelberht died (again, we do not know the cause of death), the *Anglo-Saxon Chronicle* noted a change in Viking tactics, a change that was the first signal that the sea raiders had begun to see themselves in a new light: as conquerors. For rather than make a quick dash for plunder, the Vikings set up fortified camp on the

Isle of Thanet, which at that time really was an island, separated from the rest of Britain by the Wantsum Strait. The strait allowed boats safe mooring during storms and the opportunity to ride out the ebb tide, waiting for the flood tide to carry them up and into the Thames Estuary. The Isle of Thanet thus became a proving ground for the signature tactic of the new Viking incursions: the establishment of a secure base, with easy access for their boats, but one allowing rapid deployment into attack.

From their fortified base, the Vikings gave the men of Kent an ultimatum: pay up or be prepared for us to attack you at any time. The men of Kent paid, and struck a peace treaty, but the Vikings then gave notice of another aspect of their strategy that would cause no end of problems to the Anglo-Saxon kingdoms: they did not keep their word. In a society where oath taking was a key part of the social glue, the disregard of Vikings for the sanctity of oaths made them fearful opponents indeed. The Thanet Vikings ravaged eastern Kent. The fact that a few years later Canterbury Cathedral could not muster a scribe with any sort of command of Latin suggests that the attack did lasting damage. After all, for Viking raiders, human plunder was almost as valuable as bullion, for prisoners could be sold for rich prices at the slave markets in Dublin, where the Vikings had established a permanent base.

In 865, with Æthelred now on the throne, the threat to the Anglo-Saxon kingdoms escalated to a new level entirely. What the *Anglo-Saxon Chronicle* calls 'a great heathen army' landed in East Anglia. This was no longer a matter of raids for plunder and profit. The Great Heathen Army had come to conquer.

A palpable sense of shock and outrage had greeted the first depredations of the Vikings, half a century earlier. Alcuin, the great Northumbrian scholar who had been headhunted by Charlemagne to kick-start the Carolingian renaissance, wrote of his horror at the sacking of Lindisfarne:

> Lo, it is nearly 350 years that we and our fathers have inhabited this most lovely land, and never before has such a terror appeared in Britain as we have now suffered from a pagan race, nor was it thought that such an inroad from the sea could be made. Behold, the church of St Cuthbert spattered with the blood of the priests of God, despoiled of all its ornaments; a place more venerable than all in Britain is given as a prey to pagan people.[8]

Although the shock may have diminished as the attacks became regular and the anxious scanning of the far horizon for square sails and dragon-prowed boats became habitual, it still seems strange that apparently no Anglo-Saxon saw the irony of the Vikings visiting on them pretty well exactly what they had themselves done to the kingdoms of Britain four hundred years before.

What the Vikings thought, and what their motives were for this change in strategy, we do not know. The men of the north, of the lands that are now Denmark, Norway and Sweden, had their own form of writing but the strange, angular runes they carved on stone and wood tell us little; runes were mysterious, sacred, an imposition of magical meaning on to the world of men and thus not to be used for the telling of tales or the recording of history. The Vikings left it to the peoples they raided and traded to tell their story, and, not surprisingly, they told it in a lurid style. Much effort has been spent by scholars over recent decades to reclaim and reimagine the Vikings, so much so that for a time there was a danger of the Viking incursions being rewritten as a giant trade expedition that went tragically wrong. However, some balance has returned and alongside a proper appreciation of the Viking achievement is the acknowledgement that at the centre of their culture was a capacity to inflict psychopathic levels of violence.

Thus far, the violence the Vikings had been able to inflict had been limited by the small numbers in their raiding parties and the modest ambitions of their targets. But the Great Heathen Army brought numbers – estimates vary but it seems certain it ran into the thousands – and commanders who had carefully thought through their strategic goals and how they were to accomplish them. And, having landed, the Great Army, like a dragon, fed.

Edmund, king of East Anglia, had bought peace with the Great Heathen Army, but the price of peace was winter food for his guests, the usual 'gifts' required by Viking chieftains, and horses. Lots and lots of horses. For another aspect of the new strategy was to be the combination of land and sea forces, and for that to be effective the Vikings needed mounts, far more than they could transport oversea. For a full year the Great Heathen Army fed and swelled its numbers, drawing in new boatloads of raiders either fresh from the Scandinavian heartlands or seeking fresh fields as the Franks stiffened their defences. The Anglo-Saxon kingdoms watched, nervously, but did nothing. The army was too big and too forbidding to attack and there was always the hope that the dragon boats would slip away as quietly and swiftly as they had come. As guests, albeit imposing ones, in East Anglia the Vikings did no more than the usual harm of large groups of soldiers in quarters. There were no attacks on monasteries and life went on much as usual, although no doubt the men and women who drew food from the ground were pressed all the harder in providing for the extra mouths.

Such an army, such a change in strategy, required exceptional leadership and the Great Heathen Army was led by three remarkable men, reputedly brothers and sons of the legendary Ragnar Lothbrok ('Lothbrok' means 'hairy trousers'). Halfdan, Ubba and Ivarr the Boneless were their names, and they were, individually and collectively, to cast baleful shadows over the sea-fringed lands of north-western Europe. Twelve years later, the same Ubba, flying the Raven banner of the sons of Ragnar, would land on the beach at Lynmouth, ready to cut off Alfred as he fled towards the west, and thus deliver the *coup de grâce* to the final Anglo-Saxon kingdom, only to fall before the sudden counter-attack of the men of Devon. Halfdan lived a year less, finally killed in 877 by fellow Vikings in Ireland in settlement of a blood feud.

Ivarr the Boneless was the leader of the sons of Rothbrok, a man that even *The Tale of the Sons of Ragnar* calls cunning, cruel and cold. His epithet remains a mystery – *The Saga of Ragnarr Lodbrók* says he was born with gristle instead of bone, but it seems inconceivable that a man so handicapped could lead a Viking army. Ivarr kept his eye upon the further reaches of his sea kingdom, regarding the lands he conquered in England, Scotland and Ireland of a piece. He withdrew from the leadership of the Great Heathen Army after it had subjected most of the Anglo-Saxon kingdoms to its rule, returning to Dublin to forge a sea empire and dying there around 873.

The father of the leaders of the Great Heathen Army, Ragnar Lothbrok (Ragnarr Lodbrók in Old Norse), is a figure who merges myth and history, melting from the horrified report of chroniclers into the songs of skalds (the court poets and oral historians of Viking kings) and back again. Whether he ever even existed is disputed by some historians, who contend that, like Arthur, he was a figure who subsumed the tales of others into his own legend. Indeed, in tales Ragnar brought such carnage and died so often that he seems more like a figure in a Hollywood film than a man from real life. But one of the stories that attached to him would be used to explain the actions of the Great Heathen Army when, after its year-long slumber, it snapped into action. In the *Tale of the Sons of Ragnar*, an Old Norse story, Ragnar meets his final end when he is defeated in battle by King Ælla of Northumbria and thrown into a snake pit. When the Great Heathen Army moved, it moved on the kingdom of Northumbria.

Even if the ultimate motive was filial revenge, the proximate reason was the endemic civil crisis that had gripped Northumbria for the previous three years, as war flared between the rival claimants to the throne: Ælla, the supposed killer of Ragnar and, according to the *Anglo-Saxon Chronicle*, the usurper of a throne that rightfully belonged to the other contestant in the kingdom's civil strife, Osberht. Over the next decade and a half, the leaders of the Great Heathen Army would demonstrate a finely tuned sense of where the greatest political weakness lay among the Anglo-Saxon kingdoms and how best to exploit those weaknesses. Their intelligence gathering, whether from trade or captives or espionage we do not know, must have been exceptional, as was their ability to exploit this knowledge.

The Great Heathen Army had slumbered through the spring and summer of the year 866, not stirring from its lair. The sun had begun its long retreat in the sky, the trees were shedding their leaves and, as far as the kings of the Anglo-Saxon kingdoms were concerned, the campaigning season was over. Time to hunker down through the cold and the dark. But that was when Ivarr, Halfdan and Ubba led their men north, swinging 180 miles up along the Roman roads that had the city of York as their northern node, and sailing up the coast, riding the tide up the Humber estuary before rowing up the River Ouse. On 1 November 866, All Saints' Day, when the venerable churches of York would be packed with pilgrims and with all the wealth that successive kings of Northumbria had lavished upon God on display, the Great Heathen Army attacked. Even if the Northumbrians had been keeping a wary eye on the Vikings in East Anglia, they would not have expected an attack so late in the season, while the Vikings had, in their raiding through Europe, learned to use the ecclesiastical calendar to their advantage. The haul, in gold and silver and slaves, must have been great indeed, and the city, from which Constantine had been proclaimed emperor of Rome, now fell into the hands of the Great Heathen Army. Where before, having raided, Vikings would have left, this time they stayed. This was no raid, and York was a carefully chosen first target.

With its river location and access to the North Sea, the city was ideally situated for sea raiders intent on becoming sea kings, while its importance in the Roman past put York at the centre of the road system in the north of the country. Vikings had traded and met with the Northumbrians for centuries – a skeleton that archaeologists excavated recently in Bamburgh belonged to a seventh-century woman of high status who had been born and raised in Norway before she eventually died in Northumbria. It was probably those trading links that had alerted Ivarr and his brothers to the civil strife in Northumbria in the first place.

Although they had taken the city, the sons of Ragnar had not captured either of the rival kings of Northumbria. Faced with the threat to their kingdom, Osberht and Ælla came to terms and gathered the men of Northumbria to attempt to retake York and drive the Vikings from their land. It took them many months to gather the troops, all through the winter and into the spring, but the deposed kings of Northumbria intended to attack in overwhelming numbers. The Vikings were professional soldiers, so Osberht and Ælla knew they had to make up for the lack of finesse of their own troops with weight of numbers. Employing the Vikings' own tricks back on them, the Northumbrians attacked on 23 April, which was Palm Sunday. The sons of Ragnar would not expect an attack on such a major Christian festival.

At first, the assault went well. Those Vikings caught outside York were cut down and slaughtered and the walls of York, which might have made an insuperable barrier, had not been repaired during the months of Viking occupation, leaving gaps through which the victorious Northumbrians poured into the city.

And there, amid the narrow alleys and streets of York, where numbers no longer counted for it was impossible to bring their weight of men to bear, the Northumbrians were cut to pieces. Eight ealdormen died, and King Osberht too. The usurper King Ælla died as well, either in the bloodbath or, according to later tales, once captured in battle, when he was supposedly brought before the victorious Ivarr, who took a long and bloody revenge on him by sacrificing him to Odin through the rite of the blood eagle.

Northumbria, during the seventh century the most powerful kingdom in the land and the cradle of a scholarly renaissance that had transformed north-western Europe, was destroyed. Although Anglian earls continued to rule the northern half of the kingdom from their stronghold on the coast at Bamburgh, they were cut off from the rest of the Anglo-Saxon kingdoms and essentially ceased to play any role in Anglo-Saxon affairs (although the earls did later act as kingmakers in the power politics of the Viking kingdom of York, playing a crucial role in bringing down the last great Viking king of York, Erik Bloodaxe, in 954). The sons of Ragnar had achieved their first objective.

Showing a lightness of touch that would not always be their hallmark, the sons of Ragnar installed a puppet king, but one that conveyed legitimacy, on the throne in York and settled down to summer in the north, while the other Anglo-Saxon kingdoms nervously waited to see if one kingdom would be enough to sate the dragon.

It was not. In the autumn of 867, the Great Heathen Army rode into Mercia. Although Wessex had lately supplanted Mercia as the most powerful of the Anglo-Saxon kingdoms, it remained rich and populous. Having virtually no coastline, the Mercians had escaped lightly from the Viking raids of previous years and perhaps King Burgred had hoped that the sons of Ragnar would balk at taking a kingdom with so little in the way of obvious moorings. But rivers were as good as roads for the Vikings, and Mercia was bounded and bisected by navigable rivers, allowing the sons of Ragnar to employ their favoured tactic of combined land and amphibious operations. Before King Burgred could summon his forces, the Great Heathen Army had taken Nottingham. Easily defensible, the town lay on the River Trent, and was thus accessible from York by land and water. And there, dug in, with their boats ready should a rapid retreat be called for, the Vikings waited for a response.

King Burgred called for help. He sent messengers to his ally, Æthelred, king of Wessex, asking for him to come with his forces to face the Great Heathen Army. As Æthelred received the messenger, most likely with his brother Alfred standing beside him in hall, it must have been clear to both young men that this Viking threat was different from the raids of previous decades, and required a united response from the Anglo-Saxon kingdoms. When King Burgred's messenger rode north, he went with the assurance that Wessex would answer Mercia's call. Alfred was maybe nineteen, the second man in the kingdom and heir apparent, and he was about to march to war.

An orphan by the age of ten, Alfred had done his growing up under the eye of his older brothers. When his father had died, there had been four brothers older than him still surviving. While fraternal strife had severely damaged the Carolingian

Empire after the death of Charlemagne, the sons of Æthelwulf managed to thrash out agreements between themselves as to the settlement of the kingdom – agreements that figured so large in memory that Alfred still referred to them when writing his will many years later – and Alfred, so far as we can tell, seems to have had as warm an upbringing from his brothers as was possible in the circumstances. The tale related by Alfred to Asser of his winning the book, over his brothers, from his mother suggests that he always had a mind turned towards more scholarly pursuits than his siblings – or, at least, that Alfred wanted to portray that image to posterity. But as the youngest of five brothers, and thus in the normal course of events a boy not expected to come to the throne, it's possible that the family had first planned for him to follow an ecclesiastical career. Certainly, Alfred's piety, his devotion to learning and his family connections would have made him a formidable bishop, but events intervened.

We have some clues as to the man Alfred would eventually become in what Alfred tells us of himself, through Asser, in these formative teenage years. Despite the tale of the memorised book, Alfred only learned to read when he was twelve, by which time he was living with his brother, Æthelbald, the one who had ousted their father from the throne. The chief training of a young ætheling lay in martial pursuits, above all hunting, which served to teach horsemanship, strategy, tactics and the marshalling of forces, as well as habituating a young prince to death and ensuring the physical strength and fitness that were a basic requirement for a king of the time. But Æthelbald must also have ensured a teacher was on hand to instruct his younger brother in his letters, although the young Alfred only learned to read and write Old English as a child. Latin, the language of scholarship, history and, most importantly for Alfred, God's teaching, would have to wait many years, he only learned to read and write Latin when he was nearly forty; testimony to Alfred's mental flexibility and unceasing desire to learn.

Although it would be many years before he learned Latin, Alfred was a diligent student. Asser tells us that he always carried a little book with him, a notebook in effect, in which Alfred copied passages that particularly struck him for later thought and study. The little book also served Alfred's daily religious devotions, for into it he had 'written the day-time offices and some psalms and certain prayers which he had learned in his youth'.[9] 'Office' here does not refer to a room with a desk and stylus and David Brent, but rather the daily prayer of the church, mainly derived from the Psalms of the Old Testament. Alfred prayed, dutifully and prayerfully, every day, and this is a key insight into his character: he was a fundamentally religious man, who strove to bring his life, in all its aspects, into conformity with his faith. This attitude had its origins in his youth when, faced with the eruption of sexual desire and the struggle that brought him, he prayed earnestly that God might send him some sort of physical affliction that would temper his soul and take his mind from temptation. In a stark reminder that you must always be careful in what you pray for, God sent Alfred piles! At a time when a great deal of an ætheling's life was spent on horseback, this must have been excruciating for Alfred, although it seems to have been effective in distracting him from further temptation. Alfred, mindful that God, according to the letter to the Hebrews, 'scourgeth every son whom he receiveth' (Hebrews 12:6), attempted to endure the pain and accept it as punishment and restitution. But even Alfred in the end found the pain and humiliation attendant upon piles too much and, having prayed that God would send him a physical distraction from sexual desire, he prayed that God would take away that particular distraction and give him some less severe illness, and one that didn't leave physical marks on the body, as an ætheling with leprosy or rendered blind would be useless as well as helpless. Having learned greater specificity in his prayer life, Alfred's plea was answered, and the piles disappeared. However, some years later, and most unfortunately for Alfred, his prayer was belatedly answered. During his wedding feast, when Alfred was twenty years old, he was struck down by a disease that would afflict him for the rest of his life, and it was indeed one that left no physical mark and, although severe enough for Alfred to scour the world for a cure, even corresponding with the patriarch of Jerusalem, it did not debilitate him. From this distance it's obviously impossible to be absolutely confident what the illness was, but the diagnosis that best fits the description – a chronic condition with periods of remission, agonising pain in the stomach, blood in the stool, depression, fatigue and onset as a young adult – is Crohn's disease, an inflammation in the lining of the digestive system. The condition, whether it was Crohn's disease or something else entirely, continued through the rest of Alfred's life and cast a long shadow of suffering over his years. In the days before medicine could offer any treatment for a chronic condition, the only hope lay in prayer and, when prayers were not answered, stoic acceptance of pain and the laying of suffering at the foot of the Cross, that it might in some way join with Christ's saving sacrifice.

Alfred's lifelong affliction flared up for the first time on his wedding day. Although the fact that he later fathered five surviving children as well as a number of others who did not make it out of childhood shows that, once married, he did not repress the sexual side of his nature, the fact of the disorder starting on the day of his wedding feast suggests that at heart Alfred was torn between secular and sacred callings. As the fifth son, and one with bookish inclinations, he may well have been intended, and personally inclined towards, a clerical career. Events, and the death of his brothers, made that impossible: Alfred would rule, and a vital aspect of being king was to produce heirs. But his wedding marked the final end of what may have been a heartfelt wish to be a clerk (in the medieval sense of ordained scholar) and his irrevocable commitment to the secular life. Alfred was not yet king, but all his brothers bar Æthelred were dead. There was no other course, and the marriage helped to cement the alliance between Wessex and Mercia, for it was when Æthelred and Alfred answered the call of Burgred, king of Mercia, and marched with the men of Wessex to Nottingham to lay siege to the Great Heathen Army that the marriage was contracted.

The marriage was successful, so far as is possible to say; the siege was not. First, the marriage (although it came after the siege). King Burgred of Mercia had already married Alfred's older sister, Æthelswith. In 868, 'King Alfred, at that time accorded the status of "heir apparent", was betrothed to and married a wife from Mercia, of noble family, namely the daughter of Æthelred (who was known as Mucil), ealdorman of the Gaini'.[10] Her name was Ealhswith and we know even less about her than Alfred's mother – in keeping with the tradition that Alfred told Asser, Ealhswith did not witness any charters; she was the king's wife, not Queen of Wessex. Ealhswith lived three years longer than her husband, and was buried beside him. Though she leaves virtually no mark in the historical record, there seems an unmistakeable trace of the mark she left on Alfred by the fact that, in his will, he left her the three estates – where he was born and where he won his two greatest victories – that were the most personal to him.

Back to the siege. With Northumbria won, the sons of Ragnar had marched and sailed the Great Heathen Army south, taking Nottingham and settling down behind its walls, with the River Trent an escape route at their backs. Burgred, with the forces of Mercia, and Æthelred and Alfred, accompanied by their households and the levies of the men of Wessex, arrived outside the city and waited. The Vikings within refused to come out, and neither the army of Mercia nor of Wessex had the engines, siege craft or soldiers to storm the walls. Their only option was to attempt to starve the Viking army into submission. But the winter was drawing in. Ivarr the Boneless had timed his assault on Nottingham to coincide with the harvest being taken in and supplies stored for the lean months ahead; the cupboard within the city was as full as ninth-century agriculture would allow. What's more, he was also able to draw supplies upriver from the Trent's outflow into the Humber. The situation for the besiegers was much harsher. Forced to camp outside the city, the countryside around was rapidly picked clean. With their men beginning to go short of food, and the levies – who were, after all, basically farmers taken from their fields – chafing to go home, there was little Burgred, and Æthelred and Alfred, could do. Secure, and presumably much drier than the men outside the walls, all Ivarr had to do was wait.

He did not have to wait too long. With his men drifting away, Burgred had to come to terms. The *Anglo-Saxon Chronicle* simply states that 'the Mercians made peace with the army'.[11] But peace came at a price, and one that Burgred would have had to measure out, under the suspicious eyes of the sons of Ragnar, as he gathered the hundreds, maybe thousands, of ounces of silver that the Vikings demanded for their peace.

It was a humiliation, and an expensive one at that, but it bought time. Ivarr, content with the takings from a couple of months spent in relative comfort in Nottingham, led his forces back to York. Alfred, with his new bride, returned to Wessex. Burgred, his realm weakened and poorer, looked nervously north to where the Great Heathen Army, returning to the threatening somnolence that had marked its first year in England, waited. Æthelred had answered Burgred's call the first time, but would he rally again after the debacle at Nottingham? At least Burgred had strengthened the alliance as best he could through the marriage of Alfred and Ealhswith.

Through most of 869 the Vikings bided their time. Their march from East Anglia to Northumbria had already brought them valuable intelligence about the rivers, roads and tracks of the country they were setting out to subjugate, and the feint to Nottingham had revealed much about the limitations of Mercian power. The only kingdom remaining of which they had little intelligence was Wessex, and the sons of Ragnar no doubt drew informers – disaffected nobles, runaway slaves, exiles and criminals – to them in York with the prospect of silver and the promise of mercenary troops in the throne struggle that preoccupied many Anglo-Saxon noble families.

Rested and reinforced, in the autumn of 869 the Great Heathen Army moved out once again. The kingdom of Northumbria had already fallen to the sons of Ragnar, and their previous expedition south had shown them the weakness of the kingdom of Mercia, but Ivarr made no effort to exploit that weakness at this time. Instead, following the Roman roads, while simultaneously deploying his seaborne troops, Ivarr fell upon Peterborough, sacking the abbey and killing the abbot and monks. The Great Heathen Army had made its decision. From Peterborough it turned east, upon the kingdom where it had first landed and which had first bought it off. Ivarr had decided to destroy the kingdom of the East Angles.

What happened next is all too clear in its outcome, but shrouded in legend as to its detail. The Great Heathen Army killed King Edmund and took East Anglia. That is certain. But whether the king died in battle, cut down by the Vikings, or gave himself peacefully over into their hands as a martyr for his people is not so clear. The *Anglo-Saxon Chronicle*, terse as always, states:

This year the army rode over Mercia into East-Anglia, and there fixed their winter-quarters at Thetford. And in the winter King Edmund fought with them; but the Danes gained the victory, and slew the king; whereupon they overran all that land.[12]

But there is a reason there's a town called Bury St Edmunds in Suffolk today, and King Edmund is that reason and his death was what turned him into a saint. The legend of his death was written a century later by Abbo of Fleury, a French monk who spent two years in England, where, according to his life of Edmund, he heard the story of the king's martyrdom. For if Abbo's account is correct, it was certainly a martyrdom, and thus another response drawing from the wells of Christian tradition to the whirlwind of destruction that the Northmen had brought to the land. In his prologue, Abbo says that he heard the story of Edmund from an aged bishop, who had himself heard it from Edmund's armour bearer. Whether it is true or not, the cult of St Edmund the Martyr spread very quickly after his death, so much so that the children of the men who had killed the king issued coins with his image upon them. Maybe, in the end, Edmund had his victory after all.

According to Abbo, this is what happened. Ivarr, with overwhelming force behind him, sent a messenger to Edmund calling on him to submit, to accept his status as a vassal to Ivarr and, most importantly from the Viking perspective, hand over his 'hidden gold-hordes'.[13] The alternative, as the messenger also pointed out, was death. To the pragmatic mind of Ivarr, he was making Edmund an offer the king could not refuse, while ensuring a smooth transition of power into his own hands; simpler, more efficient and, all round, better for business. But Edmund did refuse, and he sent the messenger back with an ultimatum of his own, one issued in weakness but with a ring of, to the Viking, supernatural power to it. Edmund made a challenge to Ivarr's gods, and asked of the Viking what victory was worth.

Never in this life will Edmund submit to Ivar the heathen war-leader, unless he submit first to the belief in the Saviour Christ which exists in this country.[14].

Then, according to Abbo, Edmund put his weapons aside and waited, unarmed, in his hall for Ivarr to come to him. He did not have to wait long. The son of Ragnar then had his men bind and beat Edmund, before tying him to a tree and whipping him. As the king would not yield his belief, despite the pain being inflicted upon him, the enraged Vikings threw spears at him, until Edmund resembled a hedgehog more than a man. Apparently still alive, although it's hard to see how he could have survived so long, Ivarr ordered that Edmund be beheaded. Abbo himself notes the similarity of his account to the stories of St Sebastian, which does suggest a tale embellished in the telling to fit a hagiographical framework. But whether it was in battle or by beheading, King Edmund of East Anglia was dead, and the sons of Ragnar had destroyed the second of the four great Anglo-Saxon kingdoms. Not bad for four years' work.

According to our sources, Ivarr the Boneless also decided at this time that he'd done what he'd come for. As suddenly as he arrived, this great and terrible Viking leader disappears. A later chronicler states that he died not long after King Edmund, but it is possible that Ivarr took ship and, with his ally Olaf the White of Dublin, laid siege to Dumbarton Rock, the stronghold of the kingdom of Strathclyde, and fought on in the northern mists until death finally took him. However, some sources suggest Ivarr died in 873, possibly, although unusually, of natural causes. Since a place in Valhalla depended upon death in battle, this was probably not the end Ivarr was looking for.

Although Ivarr had departed the Great Heathen Army, the sons of Ragnar were not yet finished with the kingdoms of the Anglo-Saxons. Ivarr's brother, Halfdan, took over command, with another warlord named Bagsecg, and, in keeping with what was becoming their accustomed practice, after replenishing supplies and recruiting new warriors through most of 870, the Great Heathen Army moved out of East Anglia in the autumn. Having destroyed East Anglia and Northumbria, and neutered any threat from Mercia, there was only one Anglo-Saxon kingdom left. And, as inexorably as the tide, the Great Heathen Army now moved against Wessex. Facing them were the two surviving sons of Æthelwulf: Æthelred, now probably in his mid-twenties, and Alfred, who was around twenty-one. The two brothers were about to be tested in the fire of battle as no other Anglo-Saxon leaders had been before.

4

The Year of Battles

After the legions left Britain in AD 410 it took the Anglo-Saxon invaders over two centuries to, very gradually, consolidate their hold over the territory of the displaced Britons, who were gradually pushed westwards until they became the Welsh. It had taken the Viking invaders in the ninth century just five years from landing in East Anglia to conquer or subjugate three-quarters of the land the Anglo-Saxons had won so slowly. Ivarr, striking northward with his ally from Dublin, would reduce the Rock of Dumbarton, the stronghold of the kingdom of Strathclyde that had defied the attacks of the Angles and the Picts and the Gaels for generations, and drag its people away to sell in the slave markets. The islands lying to the north-west and the north-east of the mainland, the Orkney, Shetland and Hebridean islands, now had Viking lords, who turned their shoulders readily from the plough in spring to the oar in summer. To the aghast gaze of churchmen – ever the favourite target of Viking raiders for the portable wealth of their churches, in both gold and human flesh – it seemed that God rained judgement down upon the people for their sins. To the appalled Anglo-Saxon nobility, the fighting men tasked with protecting the land and the people, it must have seemed that an inexorable tide was flowing over them, as impossible to stop as a tsunami.

But, in the end, the wave receded, and although the Viking onslaught left many marks on Britain, in the end they proved to be alterations to an existing picture, rather than the erasure that the Anglo-Saxons wrought in their slow-motion conquest of England. As Halfdan, son of Ragnar and brother of Ivarr the Boneless, gathered his forces in Thetford during the darkening days of the autumn of 870, everything remained open. Should the campaign he was planning, presumably in concert with his departed brother, prove successful, then Viking lords would be effective masters of all the Anglo-Saxon kingdoms of Britain. There was only one kingdom left standing and the sons of Ragnar, ever efficient in their intelligence gathering, would have known Wessex was led by a young, untried king, with only an even younger brother left as heir should he be removed. Kill them, and the kingdom would fall, for even though Æthelred had sons, they were still far too young to lead the forces of Wessex against a man as battle hardened as Halfdan.

The seriousness of Halfdan's intent was signalled by the time of year when he, with Bagsecg, set his men marching from East Anglia. December was the dark month, when men huddled by the fire, surviving on the harvest store and waiting for spring. It was no time for war. Æthelred must have assumed that the Northmen, without the food renders of a peasant population, would need to wait out the winter before moving. But marching down the Icknield Way, while sending his ships around the marsh meres of East Anglia to ride the tide up the River Thames, Halfdan headed straight for the royal estate at Reading. As a royal estate, the food renders due to the king would have been stored there: the threshed wheat from harvest, the salted meat of animals slaughtered through the blood month of November. It must have seemed an ideal target, and it duly fell to Halfdan. In keeping with their normal practice, the Vikings immediately set about fortifying their base, constructing 'a rampart between the two rivers Thames and Kennet'.[1] The Kennet runs south-east from its confluence with the Thames; cutting a ditch and bank between the two rivers provided an excellent landward defence while the boats pulled up on the river bank provided a retreat route should it prove necessary. The position on the Thames also meant that it was a straightforward matter for reinforcements to reach Halfdan.

How many men Halfdan led in his attempt to conquer Wessex is impossible to say for certain. It's likely some of the men of the original Great Heathen Army had already drifted away, content with their spoils, but the relative peace recorded in mainland Europe during the army's campaigns suggests that many Viking bands set sail over the channel to join with the sons of Ragnar, so there was likely to have been a steady stream of replacements for the men killed or sated. A Viking war band had to live off the land, which meant taking what they needed from the farmers and landholders in the vicinity. Foraging parties were a vital part of an army's logistics, so within three days of arriving in Reading, Halfdan dispatched a raiding party, led by two earls, to plunder and gather intelligence of the locality.

Through their campaigning so far, the Vikings had always had time, following their initial attack, to consolidate their position, as the process of summoning the local levy of men to fight generally took a great deal of time. But on this occasion the West Saxons had reacted quickly. The ealdorman of Berkshire, slightly confusingly called Æthelwulf, the same as Alfred's father, called the fyrd, the fighting men of Berkshire, together extremely quickly and, seeing the Viking force, he attacked.

Thus far, the Great Heathen Army had not faced any significant setbacks, and maybe it was that confidence that caused the earls leading the raiding party to give battle rather than retreat to the safety of the ramparts at Reading. But in the heaving, hacking scrum of the shield wall, one of the earls, named Sidrac, fell, and with a leader dead, and most likely a gaping hole opening up in the shield wall around his body, the Vikings, for the first time, broke, and fled.

Although probably little more than a skirmish, any victory, after the long parade of defeats, must have heartened the West Saxons. The conflict was duly dignified with the name the Battle of Englefield. The swift reaction by the ealdorman of Berkshire is made clear by the fact that, four days after the battle, Æthelred, with Alfred and the general levy of the men of Wessex, arrived at Halfdan's fort in Reading.

Seeing the advantage accrued to the Vikings by their being given time to prepare defences, the king of Wessex had evidently decided to face the invaders as quickly as he could. But Æthelred's and Alfred's assault on the Viking base at Reading did not go as planned:

Four days after these things had happened there, King Æthelred
and his brother Alfred combined forces, assembled an army,
and went to Reading. When they had reached the gate of the
stronghold by hacking and cutting down all the Vikings whom
they had found outside, the Vikings fought no less keenly; like
wolves they burst out of the gates and joined battle with all
their might. Both sides fought there for a long time, and fought
fiercely, but alas, the Christians eventually turned their backs,
and the Vikings won the victory and were the masters of the
battlefield; and the Ealdorman Æthelwulf mentioned above
fell there, among others.[2]

Later sources suggest that the royal brothers only just made
it away with their lives, fleeing east and making good their
escape because their local knowledge allowed them to find a
little-known ford across the River Loddon.

The optimism of the first victory in the war for Wessex had
proven short lived, and Æthelred and Alfred had learned a
painful lesson: never to underestimate their enemies, and to
always have a retreat route available. It was an expensive
lesson though, not least in the loss of Ealdorman Æthelwulf.
A man held in high regard, his body was not left to rot on the
battlefield but secretly recovered and taken north, to his home
in Derby, to be buried.

As Æthelred and Alfred regrouped their forces near Windsor,
they must have given long, hard thought to the reasons for
their defeat. Foremost is likely to have been the fact that not so
many Northmen were killed in the Battle of Englefield as they
had thought, leaving Halfdan with his forces mostly intact. It
was also possible that reinforcements had arrived upriver in

the four days between the battles of Englefield and Reading. Finally, the Vikings were skilled at defending fixed positions; although we cannot know for certain, one possibility is that there were a number of exit points to the ditch and ramparts the Vikings had built to defend their camp at Reading, and while the Anglo-Saxons were engaged in battle in one area, a flank attack originating from another exit had caught the men of Wessex unprepared. The account suggests that, even in defeat, the West Saxons had given a good account of themselves. If Halfdan and his brothers had assumed that the terror inspired by their attacks elsewhere would be sufficient to cow the final kingdom of the Anglo-Saxons, they had been disabused of the notion. But, given the tendency for Anglo-Saxon resistance to collapse after one or two reverses, Halfdan would have been confident that another victory would be enough to bring Wessex to its knees.

So, as Æthelred and Alfred had sought to follow up their success at the Battle of Englefield quickly, now Halfdan and Bagsecg determined to press home the advantage they had won at the Battle of Reading. Four days later, still in the depths of midwinter, the armies faced each other once again, at a place called Ashdown. This was the old name for the Berkshire Downs, which stretch from Reading to Marlborough, so while it gives us a general location it doesn't tell us the exact site of the battlefield. Military historians, trying to read forwards from the information provided in the texts and backwards by walking the ground and applying military logic, have suggested Lowbury Hill and Kingstanding Hill as possible battle sites, but the argument remains unresolved today. However, the place where the battle took place was well enough known in Alfred's day for it to be pointed out, possibly by the king himself, to Asser, his bishop and biographer. Asser describes the location:

> A rather small and solitary thorn-tree (which I have seen for myself with my own eyes) grew there, around which the opposing armies clashed violently.[3]

Of all the battles Alfred fought, we have the most information about the Battle of Ashdown, which suggests that it loomed large in the king's own memories. Alfred was still young, in his early twenties, and Ashdown was remarkable in a number of ways: for its victory (and Anglo-Saxon victories were rare indeed at this time), for it being the first time where Alfred clearly took command and played a crucial role in battle, and for the toll it took on the high command of the Great Heathen Army.

It was cold. The Great Heathen Army had marched from its Reading stronghold at dawn – at that time of the year the sun rises late, so the army could not have started much before eight in the morning. Heading east from Reading, into the Berkshire Downs, the Great Heathen Army's scouts had probably reported back to Halfdan and Bagsecg the location of the West Saxon forces. Both sides knew that the Great Heathen Army needed to resupply, so it's likely that Æthelred and Alfred deliberately placed their men to interdict the route to the royal vill nearest Reading – each royal estate generally being placed a day's journey apart. Æthelred and Alfred had an estate at Wallingford, and there was a large and rich monastery nearby too. It was a resource the king of

Wessex could not afford to give up without a fight, and one the Vikings required to maintain their army in the field. It also had the advantage, from Halfdan's point of view, of allowing him to move his ships upriver while simultaneously marching his men to trap and destroy the forces of Wessex.

Approaching the Downs, the Viking army split into two wings, one led by the kings Halfdan and Bagsecg, the other by the Viking earls. We don't know if these were standard battle tactics or not. In response, Æthelred and Alfred also divided their army, with the king of Wessex to lead his wing against the Viking kings and Alfred set to engage the Viking earls. It is not clear if Æthelred and Alfred were waiting for the Great Heathen Army, or hastened to intercept it from a different position. Since Asser tells us that the Viking forces had deployed in the higher, more favourable ground, it seems likely that the West Saxon forces were moving to catch them. The Berkshire Downs are composed of long ridges, the chalk soil ensuring free drainage even through winter rains. From Asser's description, the Great Army probably deployed along a ridge top. But, again according to Asser, King Æthelred lingered long in prayer before the battle while Alfred, facing the Viking forces, was faced with a choice: either to engage or retreat. He chose to attack. Closing up his shield wall, he charged, 'like a wild boar',[4] up the hill.

Everything was against the men of Wessex in this battle. The Great Heathen Army had the advantage of position, of the confidence coming from the beating they had dealt out to the West Saxons four days before, and the experience of professional warriors facing an untested army. But it was the Viking army that broke, and in the battle and its blood-soaked aftermath they left on the Downs the bodies of one king, five earls and many more fighting men, cut down by the triumphant Anglo-Saxons.

It was an extraordinary reverse for an army that had destroyed every major force put in its path up to then. And there are clues, in Asser's description and the laconic account of the *Anglo-Saxon Chronicle*, that tell us how Æthelred and Alfred pulled off the victory.

Throughout his biography of Alfred, Asser downplays the achievements of Alfred's brothers in favour of his hero, so much so that he does not even mention that King Æthelred, his prayers done, joined the battle too. The *Anglo-Saxon Chronicle*, which was collated and written under the auspices of Alfred, gives the first mention to King Æthelred and states that his forces killed the Viking king. So while it is certain that Æthelred and Alfred regarded prayer as a fundamental part of their strategy against the Vikings, it seems unlikely that Æthelred would have let his younger brother attack on his own while he remained on his knees. One possibility is that the brothers planned, quite deliberately, for Alfred to engage both wings of the Viking army, putting his head into the Viking vice, and then, when the shield walls were fully engaged and the possibility for manoeuvring reduced to a minimum, Æthelred would attack, the charge of his fresh men taking the Great Army completely by surprise and routing it. If so, it was a brave but risky tactic, requiring Alfred's men to hold the Vikings long enough for Æthelred to take them by surprise.

The Battle of Ashdown, and the later encounters in this year of battles, show Alfred's skill as a battlefield commander and his curious, and for the time unusual, lack of interest in promoting his own military abilities. In one of the translations that Alfred personally undertook, many years later, the king added a significant gloss to the text, revealing much of the motivation for what he did, and how he wished to be remembered:

> Look, Wisdom, you know that desire for and possession of earthly power never pleased me overmuch, and that I did not unduly desire this earthly rule, but that nevertheless I wished for tools and resources for the task that I was commanded to accomplish, which was that I should virtuously and worthily guide and direct the authority which was entrusted to me ... To speak briefly: I desired to live worthily as long as I lived, and to leave after my life, to the men who should come after me, the memory of me in good works.[5]

At this most basic level of motivation, Alfred stood apart from most other rulers of his day and, indeed, any day. For most of the kings of early medieval Britain, glory was a key aspect of their rule and the desire for fame was seen, even after the Christian conversion, as noble. The hero of *Beowulf*, which was composed somewhere between the eighth and early eleventh centuries, is concerned, not to say obsessed, with his fame, and the reputation he will leave after his death – for the pagan warrior, glory was all. That the poem should be transmitted and survive through the Christian centuries of Anglo-Saxon England is evidence that such attitudes continued after the conversion among the warrior aristocracy. Fame was certainly one of the key motives for Viking kings, enabling them to draw warriors to their service from far and wide as well as contributing to their glory after death.

But Alfred was different. Other Anglo-Saxon kings abdicated their kingship, seeking to pass their final years in prayer, which indicates that the cultural transformation wrought by Christianity had penetrated deeply into the souls of at least some members of the warrior class. However, withdrawal from the world was not an option for Alfred and it would not have suited his intensely practical intelligence. Once Alfred became king, his rule was characterised by the way he sought solutions for the problems he faced, analysing the situations in depth and then bringing all his power to bear on the solution. But as the victors of the Battle of Ashdown pursued the scattered Viking forces back to their stronghold in Reading, Alfred was not king, and there is nothing to indicate that he would have forced his way to the kingship if it had not fallen to him.

Although the Battle of Ashdown appeared a turning point from the viewpoint of the men of Wessex, the Great Heathen Army, despite its losses, was not so easily discouraged. Enough men had escaped from Ashdown for a fighting force to be reconstituted, and it is possible that the surviving king, Halfdan, drew in reinforcements from elsewhere in Britain. Just two weeks later, Halfdan faced Æthelred and Alfred in battle again, at a royal establishment called Basing, some three miles from modern Basingstoke and a day's march south of Reading, and this time the Vikings were left 'masters of the battlefield'.[6]

The opening phases of the war for Wessex had been fought through the depths of winter: four battles within a month must have left the survivors exhausted, and many men with wounds that needed time to heal. The war was not over, but both sides, by the unspoken mutual agreement that sometimes unites combatants, withdrew from full-scale confrontations. However, the Vikings, while they were secure in their base at Reading, needed to send out foraging parties through wider and wider swathes of the surrounding countryside. Even with low estimates for the number of men Halfdan had under his command, assuming hundreds rather than thousands, he would have needed a ton of grain each day to feed them, and much more for their horses. For the next two months the war became a series of desperate little skirmishes, with the trained men of Æthelred's and Alfred's households riding patrols over the Downs, trying to ambush the foraging parties before they could return to base. Alfred led many of these war bands himself, riding through the frozen countryside, honing the skills of evasion, concealment and ambush that would serve him all too well when, seven years later, he found himself the hunted, and the Vikings the hunters. These constant skirmishes also served to cement Alfred's reputation among the thegns of Wessex. Leading small groups of men in close-fought little battles, and leading them well, ensures a degree of closeness that can hardly be matched in any other way. Kingship at this time depended absolutely on the quality and quantity of the relationships the king could engender with his ealdormen and thegns. Little did he know it at the time, but Alfred was laying the foundations for his reign, and laying them well.

As the winter lifted, the war resumed. The armies met in battle at a place called Meretun, the location of which has never been satisfactorily established, in late March or early

April. Again, both armies deployed in two wings, the fight stretching long through the day. According to the *Anglo-Saxon Chronicle*, the army of Wessex succeeded in pushing the Viking forces back, even putting them to flight, but maybe the commanders of the Great Army had learned something from the tactics employed by Æthelred and Alfred at Ashdown, for somehow, despite this flight, the Vikings ended the day the 'masters of the field', having killed the Bishop of Sherborne and many other good men. Possibly the Vikings staged a fake rout, causing the Anglo-Saxons to break from their shield wall in hope of battlefield spoils, and then the Vikings reformed and cut down their pursuers – a tactic performed to devastating effect some two hundred years later by the Normans, themselves descendants of Vikings, at Hastings.

The *Anglo-Saxon Chronicle* notes, after the defeat at Meretun, that the Great Army was reinforced by a 'Great Summer Army', which landed in Reading. Intelligence of the approaching reinforcements may have persuaded Æthelred and Alfred to make a final attempt at defeating the Great Heathen Army before its numbers swelled again, but the plan failed. It is possible that the decision to engage the Vikings at the Battle of Meretun may have claimed one of the men who made it. Not long after Easter, which took place on 15 April in the year 871, King Æthelred died. All the sources are silent as to whether Æthelred died from wounds received at the battle, or succumbed to a disease he contracted through the campaigns of the winter, but now four out of Æthelwulf's five sons were dead. Although King Æthelred had had two sons, they were still too young to command the support of the witan in such desperate straits. Alfred, the sickly fifth son, the boy who had never thought he would grow up to be king, was now ruler of Wessex, the last remaining Anglo-Saxon kingdom. The Vikings, hearing the news through their agents, would have been heartened. Wessex had proved a far harder kingdom to crack than the others, but now, with a young, inexperienced king at its head, it was surely only a matter of time.

With what would have seemed perfect timing, the 'Great Summer Army' had arrived to claim the spoils from the richest kingdom of the Anglo-Saxons. Its leaders, fresh come from the Continent to feast on the corpse of Anglo-Saxon England, included a man who was to become Alfred's chief foe, eventual nemesis and, in the end, his ally and godson: Guthrum.

Alfred can't have expected a gentle introduction to his reign, and he did not get one. Within a month he faced the combined Viking forces at Wilton. The military situation had deteriorated greatly, for the Great Army had burst from its base in Reading and was now in the heart of Wessex. The *Anglo-Saxon Chronicle* states that Alfred faced the army with a small force. Even so, he had the best of the battle for much of the day until, again, the Viking forces feigned rout, and the exhausted but exhilarated West Saxons broke the shield wall to pursue, only for the men they were pursuing to reform and turn upon them. In the ninth general battle of the year – although not all of them are listed in the sources – the Great Army won the day. But though the Northmen had won most of the battles, and King Æthelred had died, they had not broken the resistance of the West Saxons. For its part, the Great Heathen Army had suffered more losses during this campaign than in all its campaigns against the other three

Anglo-Saxon kingdoms. For an army that fought for gain and profit, casualties were reaching unacceptable levels.

It was time to cut a deal.

It's hard for us today, conditioned as we are by centuries of wars fought for nations and ideologies, to understand how frequently bloody conflicts in the early medieval period ended with one side paying off the other. But for most of the era, there were no recognisable nations, only loyalties to the land men ploughed and the lords men served; there were no ideologies beyond the desire for gold and glory. Wars were fought for the most basic of reasons: conquest, land, loot. Even if the Northmen had never ridden the whale road and ravaged Britain, there would have been wars between the little kingdoms as kings jostled for power and, more importantly, fought for the gold that they required to win followers. Kings were ring givers, generous with gifts, and these gifts bound giver and receiver into a relationship of mutual dependence and understanding. For most of this era, to be a king was to fight, for warfare was the best – and sometimes only – way of raising revenue: taxation at the point of a sword.

The Vikings, although of different religion, shared a cultural background with the Anglo-Saxons. They had once worshipped the same – or very similar – gods, but that was less important than their shared understanding of kings as ring givers, and the acceptance that the getting of gold required the shedding of blood.

Trade, too, could raise the money needed for the gifts that glued early medieval society together. Many a Viking band would happily switch roles, from traders to raiders and back again, depending on the opportunities that presented themselves. The trade links of the Anglo-Saxon kingdoms with the rest of Europe were excellent, with much wealth generated by wool exports. Alfred, in this as in so much else, appears to have excelled: the terms of his will indicate that, by the end of his life, he had become exceptionally wealthy. However, the wealth of a king was different from that of other people, with a clear distinction being maintained, in Alfred's will and his practice, between his personal holdings, which he bequeathed to his dependents, and the money and estates that produced the income necessary for a king to fulfil his role, which he willed in their entirety to his eldest son and heir, Edward.

The war for Wessex had cost both sides dearly. The Great Army, fighting for profit, could not leave the field without taking some sort of profit from its dead, but by the summer its leaders had decided that the cost of fighting on was too great. For his part, Alfred desperately needed time to regroup, and probably even to rest. He had been fighting nearly non-stop for half a year, and, although a young man, his health was a burden throughout his life.

So, under flags of truce, the two sides met and hammered out a deal. One of the remarkable features of this time was how often blood-soaked warlords who had been up against each other in the shield wall a few weeks before would later come face to face and thrash things out with words rather than swords. Asser is sparing about the details of the deal, saying nothing more than that peace was made on the condition that the Great Army left Wessex. But this was a peace that was bought, in silver, and its payment drained a great deal of money from Wessex, with all the magnates, lay and ecclesiastical, having to contribute their share. Some small fraction of these payments has been discovered by archaeologists in the shape of buried hoards of hack silver and coins in Croydon, Gravesend and beneath where the south end of Waterloo Bridge now is.

Alfred had bought peace. In the autumn, the Great Heathen Army withdrew to London. The young ætheling, against all expectations, had come to the throne. Now Alfred had to see if he could keep it.

5

Buying Time

Alfred had bought peace, for a while. It had cost him and his people dearly, in lives and money, but they had survived.

As for the Great Army, it had other concerns. It spent the rest of 872 in London, recovering from the losses suffered in the campaign against Wessex and, presumably, enjoying some of the wealth the peace deal brought with it. Further profit accrued to the Great Army from Mercia, as its leaders extorted more money from Burgred, king of Mercia; London was a Mercian town and the Great Army naturally required payment in order to stay put and not go raiding in the rest of Mercia. That the sum paid over to the Great Army was huge is confirmed in a Mercian bishop's sale of an estate to pay 'the immense tribute to the barbarians in the year that the pagans were settled in London'.[1]

However, the shock of defeat was slowly wearing off the other kingdoms. Small rebellions began breaking out, the sort of little affairs where unwary Viking travellers were being picked off, or fire set to a newly made hall as its inhabitants slept. And as the Great Army tarried in the south, the Northumbrians grew bolder, deposing their puppet king in 872. The Great Heathen Army was learning that it is one thing to take, but another to hold. Rather than risk losing their first great gain in Britain, the Northmen went north in 873, moving the Great Army to Torksey, in the subkingdom of Lindsey, part of Mercia, which lay on the River Trent. Before the great drainage works of the seventeenth, late eighteenth and early nineteenth centuries, much of Lindsey, which roughly corresponds to modern-day Lincolnshire, was marsh and fen, with only a narrow neck of raised ground providing dry-shod access to Lincoln and Torksey. Lying on the River Trent, Torksey allowed the Vikings to launch combined amphibious and land operations into Northumbria, for it was a straightforward matter for their shallow-draught longboats to sail down the Trent, into the Humber, and then to row up the River Ouse to York. The Romans, in an unwitting good turn for later invaders, had cut a canal linking the rivers Trent and Witham, giving easy boat access to the Wash and thus the newly established Viking kingdom of Northumbria. It was an ideal base from which the Great Army could consolidate its conquest of three of the four Anglo-Saxon kingdoms.

Which is just what the Northmen did. Their man had been ejected from the throne in Northumbria, but the fires of rebellion in the north proved little more than sparks and were easily extinguished by putting a new man in charge. Of course, while they were busy putting down the Northumbrian rebellion, the Great Army asked for further payment from Mercia, which King Burgred had little choice but to provide.

The once faithful alliance he had had with Wessex seems to have lapsed; no Mercian aid came to Wessex during the first great Viking assault on the kingdom in 871, and Alfred sent no help to his brother-in-law as Mercia twisted beneath the Viking paring knife following the Viking withdrawal from Reading. Having chosen not to fight the Great Heathen Army when it lay besieged in Nottingham, Burgred seems to have lost the military confidence of his magnates. Nervous themselves, the magnates handed over their share of the Danegeld the Great Army required as it passed 872 in London, and dug deep again in 873 when the Army moved to Torksey. But the relentless demands eroded what confidence the magnates had in their king. So, when the Great Army turned its attention to Mercia in 873, Burgred found that he had irrevocably lost the support of the men he depended upon for his crown.

The Viking stroke, when it came, was masterful, and exhibited their ability to exploit political divisions in a kingdom to their own end. Rather than mounting a full-scale invasion of Mercia, and thus perhaps uniting king and magnates against them, the Great Army sent a raiding party, probably of around a thousand men, down the River Trent, past Nottingham, to Repton in Derbyshire. Repton was a hallowed place for the Mercian royal dynasty – the burial place of kings and the site of a principal church. And the Vikings took it. Drawing their *drakkar*, their dragon boats, up on the strand, they stormed the church and, applying the usual Viking tactical doctrine, fortified the site by digging earthworks to protect the spit of land that contained their ships and the church. Evincing a certain dry defensive wit, the party of Vikings from the Great Heathen Army incorporated the structure of the church into their defensive ditch, digging from bank to bank and with the church as a stronghold in the centre, its long, southern wall presented against any attackers.

For King Burgred, the game of thrones was up. His magnates, weary of the financial demands the king made of them to buy off the Vikings and keep his throne, abandoned him. Burgred, seeing power slip from his fingers, to his credit made no effort to cling to it. Instead, he put aside the sceptre of secular power and picked up a pilgrim's staff. Burgred was going to Rome. With Æthelswith, his wife and Alfred's older sister, ex-king Burgred set off on the long road to Rome, leaving his kingdom under the nominal rule of a Mercian named Ceolwulf. Burgred and Æthelswith lived out the rest of their lives in Italy, but the deposed king had not long for this life, and died shortly after arriving in Rome. Queen Æthelswith survived him by many years, dying in Pavia in 888.

The Great Army had now conclusively conquered the third of the four Anglo-Saxon kingdoms. They had also ensured there would be no help from Mercia when the Great Army turned its attention back to Wessex.

The archaeological investigations by Martin Biddle and Birthe Kjølbye-Biddle at Repton may also help to answer a mystery that the Anglo-Saxon sources have no particular interest in answering: why, after wintering in Repton, did the Great Heathen Army split apart, with some men following Halfdan and heading north to largely settle down in the region around York, whereas others, still hungry for conquest, took a new leader, Guthrum, and headed to East Anglia to prepare for another assault on the final Anglo-Saxon kingdom? The Biddles found a number of graves in Repton, dated through the coins buried alongside the bodies to the precise time the Great Army wintered in Repton. Their most famous find was the so-called Repton Warrior, a man between thirty-five and forty-five, buried in honour with many grave goods. The Repton Warrior had died a warrior's death, felled by a sword thrust through the eye and into his brain. Whoever killed the Repton Warrior was not satisfied to leave matters there, for the skeleton shows further cuts to the arm and a slash to the top of the left femur that would have cut off his genitals. Possibly that is why the Repton Warrior was buried with a boar's tusk between his legs: to make up in the afterlife for what he had lost at the end of this life.

However, the Biddles' most significant find may have been the mass interment west of the church. The burial mound was first opened around 1686, when a '"Humane Body Nine Foot long" surrounded by a hundred skeletons "with their Feet pointing to the Stone Coffin"'[2] was found. On re-excavating the mound, the Biddles found the bones of at least 249 people, whose disarticulated remains had once been stacked around the walls. The huge skeleton reported in 1686 had left no trace, but the Biddles found grave goods, including an axe, parts of a sword, various seaxes (the large knife that was the everyday tool of the period and carried by all sectors of society) and various fragments of jewellery, and these indicate the presence of a very high-status burial. Could this man have been Ivarr the Boneless, surrounded by the mortal remains of other warriors of the Great Army who had already died? Since Vikings did not put headstones on graves, we will never be certain, but if a war leader as dominant as Ivarr had died, it would explain in part the split that then took place in the Great Heathen Army.

Halfdan, Ivarr's brother and a man who had been campaigning in Britain since the army arrived in 865, went north with, in all likelihood, the older veterans of the army. Halfdan set himself up as king, establishing a base on the Tyne and raiding the Picts and Britons, traditional enemies of the Northumbrians. By attacking the Picts and Britons Halfdan may have been attempting to establish himself as acceptable to the remaining Northumbrian nobility, for to make the transition from raider to conqueror required that Halfdan co-opt the local powers to his service – he simply did not have sufficient men to take all Northumbria under his direct control. However, Halfdan did not long survive his brother, Ivarr. In 877 he died, possibly in Ireland and killed by fellow Vikings.

Two of the sons of Ragnar were now dead, with only Ubba of the three fraternal first leaders of the Great Heathen Army still alive.

But among the war lords who had sailed over sea as the Great Summer Army to join Halfdan in 871 there were leaders still gold hungry, and of the three named kings one swiftly became the undisputed leader of the Great Army: Guthrum. Taking those men who still had appetite to fight, he led the army south, to East Anglia, where it took up quarters in Cambridge. Three of the Anglo-Saxon kingdoms had been brought down and their wealth parcelled out to the Vikings, but there was still one, and the richest, left. It was a prize worth fighting for. But first the army waited, lying coiled about its base in Cambridge for a year as it prepared.

What was Alfred doing while the Great Army made its preparations? From the sources we have, it would seem not very much. Although his brother-in-law had been deposed from the throne of Mercia, and his sister had gone with him into exile, it seems that Alfred chose to continue dealing with the puppet king of Mercia, Ceolwulf. The *Anglo-Saxon Chronicle* is, in its laconic way, scathing about Ceolwulf, calling him an 'unwise king's thegn', but it is probable that Ceolwulf was of higher rank than that, with a genuine claim to the throne, as his accession was accepted without apparent demur by the magnates of the kingdom. Alfred co-operated with him in standardising the devalued silver currency that was jointly minted by the kingdoms of Wessex and Mercia, increasing its silver content from 20 per cent to over 90 per cent.

Perhaps Alfred really did believe that he had bought peace from the Vikings. We can see no evidence from our sources of any obvious military preparations. In the second half of his reign, Alfred would completely overhaul the logistical basis of his army, and bring about an extraordinary reorganisation of his realm; perhaps he made the first moves in that direction at this time, but there is nothing to say so. About the only indication of Alfred's future interests is where the *Chronicle* notes a sea engagement, in which Alfred fought seven sea raiders, one of which he captured. Alfred developed sea power as a part of his strategy in the years to come.

Why the inaction? Alfred was still quite young, just past his mid-twenties, and, with five older brothers, he had never been expected to become king. What little evidence we have for this period suggests that he was busy cementing his support among the magnates of Wessex in the time-honoured Anglo-Saxon manner: giving gifts of land to his thegns.

Although little may have been accomplished, it was a peaceful period in Alfred's often desperately fraught life. His eldest son, suitably called Edward the Elder, was born during this time. His first child, a daughter named Æthelflæd, had probably been born when his brother Æthelred was still alive, so she would have been a little, growing girl during these years. Along with two further daughters and another son, there were children who never made it from infancy. But from what we can now tell, few of the strategies – military, cultural or religious – that were to mark Alfred's reign after he was brought low and forced to flee into the marshes were present in its first phase. One possibility is that the ill health that dogged him through his life afflicted him particularly during this seemingly fallow period, preventing him from accomplishing much in the way of preparation for the storm that he must have known would someday break upon him and his people.

In 876, the storm broke.

The first campaign to take Wessex, led by Halfdan, had failed. Although the Great Army had left the land of the West Saxons quite a bit richer, with the silver Alfred must have paid as part of the peace settlement, it had lost far more men than the Vikings were comfortable with losing, and it had failed in attaining its strategic objective: the replacement of Æthelred and Alfred with a puppet king. How Guthrum conducted his own attack, five years later, showed that he had thought long and hard about the reasons for the first failure, and he was determined not to repeat them. The River Thames marked the division between Wessex and Mercia, and Halfdan, following the methods used by Viking raiders on the Continent, where they exploited brilliantly the way river systems delineated political divisions, had used the Thames as a wedge to attack

Wessex. But Æthelred and then Alfred had defended in depth, making use of the fact that none of the river's tributaries led into the Wessex heartlands, and thus in order to strike at the kingdom's heart the Vikings had to engage in dangerous expeditions far from the naval support they were used to.

But if Guthrum could not reach the heart of Wessex by river, he could do so by sea. Departing from his winter quarters in Cambridge at night and under the strictest secrecy, Guthrum, in the words of the *Chronicle*, 'slipped past the army of the West Saxons'.[3] Outpacing Alfred's forces, Guthrum marched – or possibly rode if he had acquired enough horses to mount his land forces – right through the heart of Wessex to Wareham, on the coast in Dorset. There he met the naval expeditionary force that had departed from East Anglia and sailed around the coast to meet him. Guthrum had acquired the perfect Viking base. It was located between the rivers Frome and Piddle (also called the Trent, but any river called Piddle should celebrate that name); it was a straightforward matter to dig earthworks to defend the base from landward assault. And if Alfred was minded to try a seaborne assault, Guthrum also had a base in the safe waters of Poole Harbour. Brownsea Island commanded the harbour entrance and allowed the majority of his ships to be beached there, completely safe from Anglo-Saxon attack. His base secure, and with his ships allowing him to slip past Alfred's attempted blockade to land raiders all around the huge expanse of Poole Harbour, Guthrum was sending a very clear message to the magnates and people of Wessex: your king cannot protect you. Alfred, sitting with his fyrd in the winter-blasted fields outside Wareham, knew that he simply did not have the men or siege-warfare techniques to attack Guthrum in his new stronghold, and that the longer Guthrum remained ensconced in the heart of Wessex, able to resupply at will via his fleet, the shakier his hold on the throne would become.

So Alfred turned to negotiation. For the Great Army, this was a tried and trusted method of turning a quick profit with minimal loss but, as events would show, Guthrum was playing a longer game with Alfred. For his part, the king of Wessex desperately needed to find a way to hold Guthrum to the treaty they were negotiating. Meeting beneath flags of truce, the Anglo-Saxon king and the Viking king both had the chance to size up their enemy. Warfare, which has today often become a detached technological video game, was in the early medieval period intensely personal – men talked one on one with their enemies and killed each other at short range. The negotiations gave Alfred and Guthrum the chance to weigh each other up; we have no record of Guthrum's appearance or manner, but a man who could command a great Viking army was unlikely to have been lacking in charisma, intelligence and physique. Alfred, if his illness was afflicting him, might not have cut such an impressive figure.

As he faced Guthrum, Alfred knew he was faced with a man who had no incentive to keep any treaty that he might sign. Anglo-Saxon society was bound together with the glue of oath taking; without a police force and with only a rudimentary judiciary, it was men's words that counted, and placing an oath before God served to ensure divine retribution on oath breakers at a time when any secular redress was, at best, uncertain. But Alfred knew only too well that Vikings were more than happy to swear oaths on the Christian God – and then break them.

So as he concluded his negotiations with Guthrum, Alfred asked that the Viking leader swear to abide by the terms of the agreement on 'the holy ring' – probably an object sacred to the religion of the Northmen – as well as the Christian relics that bound his own oath. Alfred, whatever figure he had cut to Guthrum, was trying to find a way to bind the Viking leader into the ideas of kingship and obligation that held together Anglo-Saxon society; in effect, he was attempting to assimilate Guthrum. In doing so, Alfred would have followed the usual elements in a treaty with the Vikings – payment and hostages – as well as including his new approach to oath taking. Although the sources are chary of mentioning it, there's little doubt that Guthrum would never have agreed to leave Wareham without a substantial payment in silver. Hostages were standard parts of any deal; the status and prestige of the hostages given usually depended on the relative strengths of the two sides. In this case, Guthrum had a slight advantage, so he would have been able to demand slightly more high-status hostages from Alfred than the king of Wessex could ask of him. But whatever their status, a significant number of individuals were given as surety of good behaviour.

Alfred was sure he had struck a good deal. He had Guthrum's word that he would leave Wessex, an oath made on the Viking's heathen gods as well as his own; he had hostages, and he had made the Great Army's venture worthwhile for them. Given the normal Viking preference for profit, Alfred must have been confident that he had secured his kingdom again.

But Guthrum was not after gold. He wanted a crown, and the only one left was Alfred's.

With a treaty signed and promises given of withdrawal, Alfred had allowed his siege of Wareham to slacken. The negotiations had dragged into spring and the men of the Wessex fyrd needed to get back to their farms to sow crops lest they starve later in the year. This was the weakening that Guthrum had been waiting for. In secrecy and stealth, his mounted forces slipped from Wareham and rode west, outpacing the men Alfred desperately scrabbled together to shadow them.

For the hostages Alfred had placed into Guthrum's keeping, the breaking of the treaty meant death: the Viking leader had their throats cut. Guthrum killed the hostages he held in the sure knowledge that he was also ensuring the death of the hostages that Alfred held, taken from among his own men. But Guthrum must have reckoned their loss acceptable; perhaps he had managed to remove some minor threats to his own position by carefully selecting the hostages he had given Alfred. For Alfred, walking in to Wareham and seeing the bodies of the people he had given into Guthrum's keeping must have been the most chastening of experiences. All his stratagems had come to nothing, and these people had died in consequence.

The mobile Viking land army had no difficulty keeping ahead of Alfred even though he followed them with his own mounted household warriors. The Great Army had a new objective: Exeter.

Guthrum was pursuing his strategy of demonstrating the inability of Alfred to guard his realm. Discontent among the magnates would have been further fomented by the fact that they would have had to contribute hugely to the payment

Alfred made to Guthrum at Wareham, only for their sacrifice to have proved futile.

There may have been further motive in Guthrum's move. Exeter was still the home to many native Britons. Further west, Cornwall had only recently come under the domination of the kings of Wessex, for Dumnonia, the ancient kingdom of Cornwall and Devon that had come into being following the withdrawal of the legions, had successfully resisted Anglo-Saxon expansion for many centuries (and, indeed, Cornish, a language descended from the tongue of the ancient Britons, is experiencing something of a revival today). By setting up a fortified base in Exeter, Guthrum was, at least implicitly, offering alliance and opportunity to the Cornish, and setting up another point of attack on Wessex. He may even have been in negotiation with the magnates of Cornwall and Devon, enticing them with promises and threats to join his cause. With Alfred sitting outside Exeter, such an attack would have been potentially devastating.

But Guthrum's careful strategy was about to be blown, quite literally, off course. His naval forces, making their way along the coast to join him at Exeter, were caught by a sudden storm, scattered, and, according to the chroniclers, as many as 120 ships foundered.

It was a devastating blow to Guthrum. But not, as it turned out, a final one. While the fleet's loss meant that any Cornish magnate who might have been tempted to join his cause decided to stay quiet, it was still beyond Alfred's power to bring Guthrum to battle or to storm his encampment: Viking expertise in throwing up fortifications and the lack of siege engineers among the Anglo-Saxons meant that the two sides were in stalemate; neither could destroy, or even displace, the other.

It was time to talk again.

Although Guthrum had ignored his oath, Alfred could claim, when they came face to face again, that his oath breaking had led directly to the loss of his fleet; even if Alfred did not believe in the Norse gods, he could claim providence as the author of Guthrum's misfortune. But with the loss of so many men, Guthrum was in a weaker position than when the two men had met at Wareham.

The negotiations were protracted, dragging through the winter of 876 and into 877. When they were finally concluded, Guthrum had to give Alfred as many hostages as the king of Wessex required, presumably including men the Great Army would be more reluctant to lose, as well as oaths that Guthrum, with the example of what had happened the last time he broke his word, might have been more reluctant to break. But, in the end, the terms were the same. The Vikings were to leave. But the essential relationship between the Viking and Anglo-Saxon kingdoms had not been settled: the Great Army had not given up its desire for military supremacy; Alfred, it would turn out, still sought to bring the Viking lords into the Anglo-Saxon world.

Another battle was over, but neither side was yet exhausted. The struggle continued.

Leaving Exeter, and no doubt shadowed by wary Anglo-Saxon troops, Guthrum's army rode through Wessex and on, into Mercia, their satrapy. There, Guthrum required of Ceolwulf, the puppet king, what he had promised he would provide when asked: land. For Alfred, watching from over the border in Wessex, it must have looked as if Guthrum had given up hope of taking his kingdom and settled for carving up Mercia.

Alfred had bought time. It had cost him and his people a great deal of money, but it must have looked as if his strategy had worked. The second great assault on Wessex had apparently been turned back.

6

To Kill a King

Guthrum had lost a fleet. He had renewed his oaths, given on pagan rings rather than Christian relics, and handed over hostages he was less inclined to lose. Alfred had faced him in two protracted bouts of negotiation, first with Guthrum holding the whip hand and then when he was able to enforce his own terms. Alfred knew his man well. He was confident he had beaten him. He was wrong.

As Alfred shadowed the Great Army out of Wessex in August 877, Guthrum noted the rich land his depleted army was marching through. Making his base in Gloucester, he took over the western half of Mercia from Ceolwulf, the puppet king, and began parcelling it among his chief men. This was as Halfdan had done when the Great Army split after taking Repton, leading his men up to York and dealing out the estates of Northumbria to his magnates. When news of Guthrum's actions reached Alfred, he must have felt a quiet satisfaction that he had finally seen off the Great Army.

But it appears to have been a ruse. While Guthrum handed out estates, he was also drawing in reinforcements to replace the men lost in the sea disaster that had overtaken his fleet. It is likely he also sent out messengers. Although Ivarr the Boneless and Halfdan were dead, there was another of the sons of Ragnar left alive: Ubba. After his role with the Great Heathen Army when it first descended upon Britain and then took the kingdom of East Anglia, Ubba disappears from the *Chronicle*. It seems he took his ships and men to Ireland, where the great Viking port of Dublin served as a hub for the trade in goods and slaves that drove the Viking expansion. But sometime in the later part of 877, Guthrum's messengers reached Ubba and the last of the sons of Ragnar gave his assent: he would join the final assault on Wessex.

While his messengers sailed across the Irish Sea, Guthrum had been making other preparations. His previous attacks on Wessex had depended on surprise and secrecy, and this one was to be no different. Although Guthrum had failed to drive Alfred from the throne, the king's failure to defeat the Viking lord had weakened his prestige in the eyes of his magnates. Looking north, the powerful men in the land contemplated nervously the fate of the magnates of the kingdoms of Northumbria, East Anglia and Mercia. Those who had not resisted the Great Army had generally been retained in their halls and their prestige, if not with as much power as they had had previously, but those who had resisted had been removed – either dying or fleeing. To the watching magnates, the Viking tide must have seemed inexorable: even when the Great Army suffered a reverse, fresh recruits flooded in from the Continent or the Viking homelands and it renewed its assault. Surely it was better to admit that God, for whatever reason, had deserted the Anglo-Saxons and come to an accommodation with the new overlords – after all, even the Christian bishops of the conquered kingdoms had managed to establish a working relationship with their new pagan kings. Besides, despite Asser's protestation that Alfred was 'victorious in virtually all battles',[1] in reality his most notable battlefield achievement, apart from the solitary triumph at Ashdown, was getting out alive with enough of his army intact to fight again. This, though, was no inconsiderable skill: keeping a fighting retreat from turning into a rout, particularly in the days when there were very few long-range weapons to lay down cover, is the most difficult of all military skills. That Alfred had lost so many battles in his year of battles in 871, and yet still lived, shows extraordinary battlefield ability and the absolute faithfulness of his household warriors. However, the magnates of Wessex were beginning to question their loyalty to Alfred.

From his base in Gloucester, Guthrum sent out spies, probably concealed as traders, into Wessex to keep tabs on Alfred's movements. Given the surreptitious nature of his operation we cannot be certain of its details, but hints in the records suggest that he also sent agents to at least some of the magnates of Wessex, with an offer. All they had to do was stand aside, keep their men in hall and their swords sheathed, while he made his move. It would not, after all, be a betrayal, but simply a failure to act – and the strike, when it came, would be so swift this time that there would be no blame attached to their inaction. Particularly since a new king, one more acceptable and beholden to Guthrum, would then be in place. It appears that at least one of Alfred's ealdormen gave ear to Guthrum's message: Wulfhere, ealdorman of Wiltshire and the magnate whose lands abutted the part of Mercia where Guthrum now ruled.

A charter, dating from the reign of Edward the Elder, Alfred's son and successor, states that Wulfhere 'deserted without permission both his lord King Alfred and his country in spite of the oath that he had sworn to the king and all his leading men'[2] and, as a result, had lost his position and his lands. The fact that Wulfhere appears to have escaped with his life suggests an alternative explanation: rather than actively betraying Alfred, he may have simply been too paralysed to act when Guthrum attacked and, taking fright, fled the country. Wulfhere's failure must have been a particular blow to Alfred, for he was an old and experienced ealdorman whose service stretched back through the reigns of his brothers, all the way to Alfred's father.

His plans laid, Guthrum waited for the night dark of midwinter to draw down upon the country. Alfred, with his household, repaired to Chippenham in Wiltshire for the Christmas of 877 and there he saw in the New Year as well. The Christmas feast stretched over twelve days, from the Nativity of the Lord on 25 December to the Epiphany, the celebration commemorating the visit of the Magi to the infant Jesus, on 6 January. Chippenham was a royal estate, some thirty miles south of Gloucester. Although Alfred had the men of his household with him, it seems that the other warriors of the Wessex fyrd had returned to their homes.

As he had done before, Guthrum slipped silently from Gloucester at night, and rode south, moving fast and direct for his target. Whether Wulfhere had betrayed Alfred or not,

Guthrum had definite information as to the whereabouts of the king. This time, he would strike directly at the head, and decapitate Wessex. With the last son of Æthelwulf dead, Guthrum would have no difficulty in placing his own man on the throne of Wessex. Already he had made himself king of East Anglia, and ruler of much of Mercia. Adding Wessex would put him first in glory among the leaders of the Great Army.

The attack was masterful. Not a word reached Alfred until it was too late to muster men for defence. The king of Wessex was faced with an immediate, defining, choice: to fight, and almost certainly to die in a glorious but futile last stand, or to run, ignominiously, leaving Guthrum in charge of his royal estate and sending messengers to the magnates of Wessex that their king had fled.

Alfred ran, but he did not flee. Instead, he began raiding the bases of the Great Army as it tried to consolidate its hold upon Wessex, gradually working his way westward towards the 'fen-fastnesses' of Somerset. As Guthrum heard the reports of Alfred's raids, and realised in which direction the king was heading, a grim satisfaction must have eased the frustration of having let Alfred slip from his grasp. Alfred was heading straight towards the last of the sons of Ragnar, the bearer of the magical raven banner. Ubba would cut Alfred off. Ubba would kill him, and then the conquest of Anglo-Saxon England would be complete.

But Ubba, to his surprise and the probable astonishment of all, fell beneath the swords of the men of Devon as the besieged troops of Ealdorman Odda launched a surprise attack on the Viking troops, devastating them.

Great must Guthrum's frustration have been by this point. Alfred had eluded his search parties and disappeared into the swamps of Somerset, from where he sent raiding parties, acting like Vikings, against the Great Army. The carefully planned pincer movement that was meant to cut off Alfred's retreat and block any support from the western shires of Wessex had been destroyed and, worst of all, the last of the sons of Ragnar had been cut to pieces by Saxon swords.

Whatever Guthrum did, however cunning his plans, he just could not seem to catch Alfred.

But he was to have his chance. During his months on Athelney in the Somerset Levels, Alfred had been sending messengers to the ealdormen and thegns of his kingdom, telling of his survival and summoning those who would come to stand by their king. Conscious of how Guthrum had learned of his movements, Alfred kept the information conveyed to a minimum, first calling on his men and only at the last moment telling them the where and when of the rendezvous.

Through three years, Guthrum and Alfred had danced an elaborate engagement of sieges and negotiations, but now everything was going to come down to a single battle. The king of the West Saxons and the king of the Vikings would face each other in the field of battle. The future of England lay in the outcome.

7

Out of the Marshes

Alfred celebrated Easter on Athelney, in the marshes. Few places show the new life of spring more vividly than marshland, as the dead brown rushes of the previous year's growth are pierced with the vivid green of fresh shoots, and the flat, still waters become busy with skating insect life and waking, hungry fish. For the king, the feast of the death and resurrection of Christ was a metaphor for his situation, and the plight of his kingdom. He had endured a passion, as his Lord had done; now, in the joyful weeks following Easter, he sent out messengers to the ealdormen and thegns who still proclaimed their faith to see if he too would see a resurrection.

Guthrum had struck, in speed and stealth. Alfred would do the same. Riding out on the trackways and Roman roads that skirted the Somerset Levels, the king's messengers summoned the men of Somerset, Wiltshire and Hampshire to a rendezvous in the seventh week after Easter (that is, between 4 and 10 May 878), at Egbert's Stone, a meeting place that lay to the east of the great forest of Selwood. The seventh Sunday after Easter is Whitsun, the feast of Pentecost, when in Christian belief the Holy Spirit descended upon the Apostles in fire; it was both an auspicious time for Alfred to ride from his hiding place on Athelney and it also might serve to throw off his enemies – if Guthrum had learned to make use of the Christian calendar to take Alfred by surprise, the king was not above paying him back in kind.

But as the erstwhile king rode, with the men who had followed him in defeat and stayed with him through despair to this new morning, he knew that it would all be for nothing if the men of Somerset, Wiltshire and Hampshire had not heeded and answered his summons. The fact that Alfred was able to call upon the men of Wiltshire suggests that Wulfhere, the ealdorman who was later arraigned for desertion, had fled, but that enough of the local network of king's representatives had remained loyally in place for the message to be relayed to the local people. It also reveals how tenuous Guthrum's hold on the land was. Although the Great Army held Chippenham and, no doubt, the other royal vills of the shire and possibly beyond, yet their writ barely penetrated into the hamlets and farms where the majority of the population lived. These were the men Alfred called upon now, but he had no idea if they would respond to his call. If they did not come, his cause was over; then all that would remain would be a heroic death in battle or to follow his brother-in-law, King Burgred, and to lay over the struggle and be a pilgrim.

Some 1,100 years removed in time, the emotion of that meeting, when King Alfred emerged from the track through the green dark of Selwood to see, arrayed around Egbert's

Stone, the men of Somerset, and Wiltshire, and Hampshire, still echoes through the years.

> When they saw the king, receiving him (not surprisingly) as if one restored to life after suffering such great tribulations, they were filled with immense joy.[1]

Alfred, the once and future king, had his army.

It is clear that Alfred was concerned lest intelligence of his meeting the fyrds of the three shires should reach Guthrum, for the reformed army of Wessex spent only a single night camped around Egbert's Stone. Having been on the receiving end of hit-and-run Viking raids for decades, followed by the surprise attacks that Guthrum specialised in, Alfred had learned well the principles of insurgent warfare. This time, the battle would be at a time and place of his choosing.

The day of rendezvous had been carefully chosen. Its proximity to Whitsun (possibly even Whitsun itself, although the sources do not specify the exact day), meant that it was a clear assembly date when the church's calendar was the only reliable day tracker. And while Guthrum had spent the previous few months attempting to tighten his grip on Wessex, the choice of a festival meant that men had a reason to travel away from home, and their absence was less easily marked. Presumably Alfred did not call on the men of Devon and Dorset because they had been left to patrol the coasts of Wessex against another seaborne attack. Odda and the men of Devon had already dealt a devastating blow to Guthrum's plans with their entirely unexpected defeat of Ubba, the last of the sons of Ragnar, but a wise king, aware of Guthrum's fondness for two-pronged operations, would have ensured lines of defence against further waves of seaborne attackers.

For his part, Guthrum had found the previous few months frustrating in the extreme. Having had Wessex in his grasp, it was now proving annoyingly difficult to hold. Although some of the magnates had come over to his side, others paid only lip service while waiting to see what providence brought, or the fate weavers span, and some had taken to the fen-fastnesses and forests to wage guerrilla warfare against the Great Army. Where before the great operational strength of the Viking forces lay in their flexibility and mobility, now they were tied down in the defence of fixed places, such as the base Guthrum had created at Chippenham, or they were forced to engage in patrols through a strange territory that was at best neutral and which could suddenly erupt into ambush. The best strategy for the Viking king was to gradually normalise his rule, striving as much as possible to rule through the channels that Alfred had used, suborning the ealdormen and local nobility. But with the king still alive, and present, though hidden, it was impossible to persuade the majority of the local nobility to his side. With the loss of Ubba's ships, Guthrum's chance of attacking Alfred in his marshland base had disappeared. So, through the spring, both men prepared. In the end, the fate of Wessex, and England, would come down to a single battle.

Having met his men at Egbert's Stone, Alfred did not tarry there. The next day, at dawn, not waiting for any stragglers, the army of Wessex marched north to Iley Oak, possibly in Eastleigh Wood outside the Wiltshire village of Sutton Veney. This forward location was carefully chosen, as the River Wylye protected the northern flank of Alfred's camp from sudden attack, while the king sent out scouts to ascertain Guthrum's position.

Alfred had a single strategic objective: to destroy or drive the Great Army from his land. How he did that depended, vitally, on where Guthrum and his main body of men were. If they were still in Chippenham, his course was straightforward: march on the royal vill, besiege it, and cut its communications, via the River Avon, with other Viking forces. If Guthrum was not in Chippenham, his main base, then Alfred's choice was to march directly on the Viking's main base and take it, cutting off Guthrum's line of communication, or to meet Guthrum's army directly in the field.

For his part, Guthrum's patrols must have been relaying increasingly alarming messages to him in that final week before Whitsun. Men were moving, slipping down trackways and into the forests. Rumours, ever the first but most unreliable harbingers of battle, spread widely and wildly, sending the Great Army's patrols out chasing shadows, as they had done through the frustrating months of trying to hunt down Alfred. But, as the groups of men coalesced, and Alfred met them, a Viking patrol, mounted on fast horses, must have observed them and galloped back to Guthrum. Alfred was marching on Chippenham, with an army at his back.

For Guthrum, the news must have brought more relief than trepidation. His men were professional soldiers and now, finally, they would have a chance to come to grips with the phantom that had plagued them these past months. Faced with his own strategic choice – whether to remain behind his defences at Chippenham or to march out to meet Alfred in battle – Guthrum did not hesitate. He marched. With the advantage of mobility – most of his forces had horses – he called in all the patrols that could reach him in time and set out south from Chippenham. Alfred had come out of the marshes, but Guthrum would choose the ground of their final meeting.

With his scouts reporting that Alfred was marching towards Chippenham, Guthrum reacted immediately. Leaving a small garrison in his base, Guthrum marched the Great Army south to intercept the army of Wessex. He took up position on Bratton Castle, an Iron Age hill fort on the western edge of Salisbury Plain. The old hill fort, long abandoned but with its earth banks still impressive today, rose 740 feet (225 metres) above the farmlands running north towards Chippenham (the Westbury White Horse, a chalk figure cut into the grass, lies on the side of the hill, documented from 1742). From its vantage point, Guthrum could keep watch for miles around for Alfred's army. Without a water source, it was no place for a main camp, but it was ideal for reconnaissance, and provided the high ground should Alfred be willing to close on Guthrum.

As Alfred marched north his scouts brought back their reports: Guthrum had left Chippenham and taken up position on the fort of the old people. Soon, the king could see for himself the Great Heathen Army, their spear points glinting as they looked down from Bratton Castle. Although Alfred had attacked up hill at the Battle of Ashdown, here it was out of the question; the slopes were too steep. But rather than occupying the summit of a hill, Bratton Castle lies on a long ridge. Alfred could lead his men up on to the ridge and then advance on Guthrum. But, shading his eyes to take in the enemy position,

Alfred must have grudgingly acknowledged Guthrum's field skill: by positioning himself on the narrow ridge, the Viking leader had ensured that his shield wall could not be outflanked. Thus, at one stroke, Guthrum had neutralised Alfred's chief advantage: in this battle, he outnumbered the Great Heathen Army.

The Great Army had been whittled away in the previous months, losing many hundreds, possibly even thousands, of men in the sea disaster that had overtaken its fleet sailing to Exeter. Other men had left, heading north with Halfdan to settle around York. And then, when Guthrum had taken Chippenham and, as he thought, finally conquered Wessex, he had had to send patrols of his men out to enforce his will on the people and to garrison outlying posts. Fast riders had brought back as many of those patrols and garrisons as was possible, but the speed of Alfred's approach meant that it was impossible for them all to get back in time.

For his part, Alfred had summoned the fyrds of three counties, Somerset, Wiltshire and Hampshire. Estimates vary as to how many fighting men this would entail, but 4,000 is a reasonable figure, and such a host would have outnumbered the army that Guthrum could pull together at such short notice.

However, with the narrow neck of land atop the ridge, and the careful use of the ditches marking out the hill fort, Guthrum could funnel Alfred's shield wall tight, so it could not come around to outflank him. As Alfred led his army on the long march uphill, the king would have been all too aware that the battle he was about to enter was going to be a brutal and bloody shoving match.

As the two kings dressed their lines, high above the Wiltshire Plain, they both knew this was the crucial battle. The battle-hardened warriors of the Great Heathen Army knew what they were about: they had had years of virtually unbroken conquest and, while their confidence may have been knocked by the unexpected defeat and death of Ubba, the last son of Ragnar, there was no reason for them to believe the fate weavers had started sewing a different pattern. The core of Alfred's army was made up of his personal retainers, the men who had escaped with him into the marshes and raided the Vikings through winter and spring, and the retainers of the magnates of Somerset, Wiltshire and Hampshire – man for man, as good troops as the warriors of the Great Army. But the majority of Alfred's army were not trained soldiers, but farmers and artisans, free men who owed service to their lord, and who fought for their families and their land. Such men marched to battle with whatever weapons they had to hand: spears – the mark of a free man was his entitlement to carry a spear, a slave could not; sickles and other farming implements, cudgels and knives and staves. Among these men there would be barely an item of armour, and precious few, if any, swords. As they marched towards the waiting line of Vikings, many a man must have bolstered his courage with beer, or left the column to vomit his fear away.

The Northmen waited, in solid line, their painted shields interlocked, spears prickling out through the wall like a porcupine. As the army of Wessex approached, the commanders detailed to each flank pushing the men on the inside tighter to stop the shield wall spreading, the men drummed on the rims of their shields. Boasts, insults and threats rang out as the lines closed and it became clear, to each man in the converging shield walls, whom he would face in the enemy line. This was war at its most up close and personal.

But before the lines met, Alfred's men, particularly those in the second and third lines of the shield wall, unleashed their throwing spears, javelins designed to embed themselves in a shield and, through their weight, pull the shield down and expose its holder to a spear thrust.

And, then, the clash, the coming together of the two lines, in an impact of wood, and bone, and muscle. In these battles there was none of the clouds of gunpowder smoke that would obscure later battlefields – everything was stark in its clarity. But the king could not take advantage of this clarity by standing back and directing the battle; of necessity, Alfred's place was in the centre, in the front rank, albeit protected by his best warriors, men prepared to die to save their lord. Guthrum also took his place in the front rank, flanked by men who bore the rings their lord had gifted them.

Spears with leaf-shaped heads thrust through gaps in the shield wall, aiming for eyes and faces. Other spears, with twin projections on the socket, were used to hook enemy shields and weapons, opening them to a follow-up thrust. As men died or, injured, fell back out of the line, others pushed forward to take their place – any gap opening in the shield wall could be fatal.

As the battle wore on, sheer fatigue started to play as much a part as battlefield losses. And this is likely where Alfred's advantage in manpower started to pay off. The sources tell us the battle lasted a long time, long enough for the adrenaline rush of battle to begin to wear off, long enough for even the

experienced warriors of the Great Heathen Army to begin
to flag against weight of numbers and the sheer, dogged
determination of Alfred and his men. Unlike so many other
Anglo-Saxon armies before them, they did not break and they
did not flee, but, with Alfred safe at the centre of the line and
his banner flying, the men of Wessex began to break through
the shield wall of the Great Heathen Army. As exhaustion set
in, the killing distance grew shorter, and men started using
their shields as weapons, the great central metal bosses shoved
with bone breaking force into shoulders, arms and faces. The
stragglers, the men who waited behind the lines of the army
of Wessex, fearful of joining in, seeing the Viking line begin to
open and break, started to pile in, wielding makeshift weapons
on wounded men lying on the ground, finishing them off and
stripping them of whatever they carried.

When the end came, it was probably quick. The Great Heathen
Army broke. The shield wall cracked open, the exhausted,
triumphant, blood-driven men of Wessex burst through, cutting
men down as they ran, bypassing those who retreated in good
order, shields and spears presented outwards, as the lust for spoil
and the wonder of still being alive drove them on.

Guthrum, with his ring-given men, the best and toughest
of the Great Army, retreated to the tethered horses, protected
by a small picket of men, and made their getaway. But the
rest of the Great Army fell there, cut to pieces, the riches with
which the Vikings adorned themselves, riches spoiled from
others, despoiled from them, and their dead bodies left upon
the hillside for the ravens and the wolves.

Alfred, standing, swaying with exhaustion on the hilltop,
saw Guthrum riding away.

It had all come down to this one battle, the Battle of Edington, and Alfred had won.

But Guthrum had got away before, most notably at Wareham and Exeter, when he had appeared cornered. Alfred was determined not to let that happen again. Although most of his army was on foot, Alfred and his personal retainers, as well as the magnates and their men, had horses. Leaving the rest of the army to finish off the Viking stragglers, rest and then follow behind, Alfred set off after Guthrum, cutting down any stragglers along the way. The Viking king was heading north. Chippenham, his base and Alfred's erstwhile vill, lay some twelve miles away and Guthrum reached there before nightfall, disappearing behind the earthworks and palisades his men had constructed over the last few months. Alfred took immediate steps to isolate the encampment:

> he [Alfred] seized everything which he found outside the stronghold – men (whom he killed immediately), horses and cattle – and boldly made camp in front of the gates of the Viking stronghold with all his army.[2]

Although the sources do not mention it, Alfred presumably stationed guards downriver on the Avon to prevent resupply reaching Guthrum. The Vikings appear to have made no attempt to escape by water either, so Alfred may have been able to construct some sort of a barricade to prevent boats slipping away at night, possibly by half cutting bankside trees so they fell into the river, but with part of the trunk still attached to their roots.

In effect, Alfred was laying an interdict on the land around the Viking encampment, making it impossible for Guthrum to send out raiding parties to resupply, cutting off and killing any stragglers attempting to get back to Guthrum, and preventing any supplies getting through to the besieged remnants of the Great Heathen Army.

Guthrum hung on as long as he could within his fortifications, hoping that Alfred's army, hearing the call of land and farms that needed tending, would melt away. But it did not. Alfred simply drew the siege tighter, choking off all food and supplies.

It was only a matter of time.

In the end, it took fourteen days to starve Guthrum and the desperate remnants of the Great Army into suing for peace.

The Vikings offered Alfred as many hostages as he wished, of his choice, if he would let them go. The Great Heathen Army was so reduced, and so desperate, that it did not even ask for any hostages from Alfred in return.

After years of battle, after all but losing his kingdom, Alfred had brought Guthrum down. The only question that remained was whether he should let him go, or should he seek to finish him off – kill him, and the remnants of the Great Army.

As Alfred sat among his counsellors, listening to their advice, he must have recalled the bodies of the men he had given into Guthrum's hands as hostages in Wareham. He remembered his brother, Æthelred, who died during the first great Viking attack on Wessex. He recalled all the men who had been killed in the years of struggle, the monasteries despoiled, the people herded off into slavery.

With all these reasons to hate Guthrum, yet Alfred, sitting there in council, found the strength to lay his hatred aside. He would let Guthrum go.

All these centuries later, and having walked alongside Alfred through the desperate struggle against the Vikings, the decision still seems incredible. But in that decision lies one of the reasons why Alfred really does stand as exceptional among kings. For though he distinguished himself as a war leader, it is what he did with the peace afterwards that marks him out, and it all starts from this decision. Asser is quite clear about why Alfred decided to let Guthrum live:

> When he had heard their embassy, the king (as is his wont) was moved to compassion and took as many chosen hostages from them as he wanted.[3]

The foundation and font of Alfred's life was his religion. Christianity enjoins the forgiveness of enemies. As a man who had been betrayed by Guthrum, Jesus' answer to Peter's question may have resounded in Alfred's soul:

> Then came Peter to him, and said, 'Lord, how oft shall my brother sin against me, and I forgive him? till seven times?' And Jesus said unto him, 'I say not unto thee, until seven times, but until seventy times seven.' (Matthew 18:21–22)

Alfred was enjoined to pardon his enemies, despite multiple offences on their part, and he took this seriously.

But he was also a king, a king in dangerous times, and the primary duty of a king is to protect his realm. Alfred was perfectly capable of acting ruthlessly when the occasion demanded; indeed, as Asser points out, when the king arrived at Chippenham to interdict Guthrum, he immediately executed all the Vikings caught outside the fortifications. Although the text does not tell us, the suspicion must be that the executions were staged to be clearly visible to the men inside the camp.

By letting Guthrum live, Alfred was clearly taking a risk that the Viking would retreat, regroup and attack again. How did he decide the risk was worthwhile?

Firstly, the group of hostages that Alfred took was clearly among the most notable men still surviving in the Great Heathen Army, rather than the expendables Guthrum had cheerfully sacrificed at Wareham.

The defeat Alfred had inflicted on the Great Army at Edington had also totally changed the dynamic of the war. Now, the fortunes of war, whether they were woven by the fate singers of Norse myth or the providence of Alfred's triune God, had clearly shifted to the Anglo-Saxons. In the tides of men, momentum is all, and Alfred had it. So much so that 'Guthrum, their king, promised to accept Christianity and to receive baptism at King Alfred's hand'.[4]

For Alfred this was a game changer, but even so he knew it did not come without risks. Other Viking kings had received baptism before, sometimes many times over. Some of them seemed to regard it as a professional hazard.

But the potential benefits of Guthrum's baptism were too great, in Alfred's mind, for him not to take the risk. Besides, when assessing the reasons for Alfred's decision, there is one factor we cannot account for at our range: the fact that Alfred knew his enemy. He had negotiated with him, face to face, on at least two occasions before the Viking's capitulation at Chippenham. He had been lied to by Guthrum, betrayed by him, and now he saw the man brought low and as close to begging for his life as a Viking king could come. Alfred knew the man now, knew when he lied and when he told the truth, and the king judged that this time – this time – Guthrum's eyes were clear of lies.

The Viking Age was a time when gods contended in the clash of swords – for both sides, the earthly victor was a reflection of the celestial struggle. For seven years, and through two great campaigns, the followers of Thor and Odin One-Eye, Lord of Battles, had attempted to drive Alfred from his kingdom, or, more simply, just to kill him. And, always, they had failed – even when they had taken his kingdom, the king, like a ghost, had returned and inflicted a crushing defeat upon them. In the clash of gods, it was clear to Guthrum, and Alfred, that the God of the Christians had triumphed over the gods of the Vikings. As such, Guthrum's decision to embrace Christianity was probably quite heartfelt – he wanted some of that strong magic that had defeated him when the prize was in his grasp.

For Alfred, the baptism of Guthrum meant that the pagan Viking would be infused with God's spirit, the same fire that had filled the Apostles on the Pentecost feast when he himself had ridden from the marshes and met his people at Egbert's Stone. Such an infusion meant transformation – possibly. Alfred was not so naive as to believe that the grace of baptism brought an inevitable change, but he himself had seen and read examples of men's lives shattered and reformed through the acceptance of a new belief, so he was alive to the possibility.

But there were other considerations that informed Alfred's decision to accept Guthrum's conversion and let him leave Chippenham, alive and still in command. The only way to have exterminated the remnant of the Great Army that Guthrum still commanded was to kill them – faced with a refusal to negotiate on Alfred's part, the Vikings would have realised their only recourse lay in attempting to break out. They would have been beaten, defeated and destroyed, but the killing of them would have cost Alfred dear in his own men's lives too. Alfred needed his soldiers – everything he had learned of the Vikings told him that someday there would be more raiders and more armies scudding over the horizon.

This premonition that there would be more raiders gave Alfred further incentive to keep Guthrum alive and in charge, so long as he could bring the Viking into the Anglo-Saxon network of obligations. As Alfred and his counsellors met to discuss Guthrum's offer of hostages and conversion, somebody, possibly the king, pointed out that killing Guthrum would have simply left a vacancy at the top of the Viking tree in Britain, a vacancy that would soon be filled by another man needing gold and glory, and thus conquest, to hold his position. Leaving Guthrum in place, tethered, bought Alfred an ally among his enemies, a policeman to hold the more unruly visiting Vikings in check. Alfred had defeated Guthrum through the hard power of the sword; now he sought to co-opt him through the soft power of religion and culture.

For Guthrum, the decision to accept baptism was no less far reaching and probably quite as calculated. Alfred's God had proved superior to his own gods, but entering Christianity and taking Alfred as his godfather meant that, while he accepted a subordinate position to Alfred, he would remain a king, of East Anglia, and have a defined place in Anglo-Saxon society. As king, the riches that had attracted Vikings as raiders would be bestowed upon him as ruler; the rich estates and trade of the East Angles would flow into his hands and be available to give as gifts to his retainers and thus ensure their continued support. Defeat dimmed the glory that attracted men to a Viking lord's banner, but gold and silver could serve just as well to recruit and retain men who fought for profit as well as reputation.

So Guthrum would become a Christian king. In that, he would be supported by the only remaining Saxon king in Britain, but now indubitably the most powerful one, Alfred. It was an extraordinary turnaround, and one that the Viking lord had chance to reflect upon as he and thirty of his chief men rode with Alfred along the trails and ways that led into the king's marsh fastness. For his baptism, Alfred took Guthrum to Aller, near Athelney. There, near the site of his lowest fortune, Alfred brought the Viking chief into communion with himself and his God. To ensure the acquiescence of Guthrum's men in the new dispensation, Alfred (and no doubt Guthrum too) insisted that the thirty greatest among them be baptised as well.

The church in Aller is surrounded by farmland nowadays, but the level land hints at the marsh that once surrounded the slightly raised church. As the thirty white-clad Northmen processed towards the church, and stood waiting to enter, a priest exorcised the evil spirits that had dwelled in them by blowing upon their faces. Once inside the church, each man had to renounce his errors – his gods – of old. They were then signed with the cross, and salt, the savour of divine wisdom, was placed upon their tongues. The men, with Guthrum leading, were then taken to the font – most likely they were completely immersed in water, so the font must have been large indeed.

Guthrum was immersed three times, emerging each time for the cross to be signed upon his forehead. The hand upon his shoulder, as he emerged from the water, was that of Alfred, his godfather, his king, his ally. As the Viking chief emerged for the final time from the water, he was a pagan lord no longer, but Æthelstan, the Christian king of East Anglia. As the sight of the erstwhile Viking cleared, he might have reflected that he had not done too badly after all. The ultimate prize of Wessex had eluded him, but he was alive, he remained the most powerful Viking lord in the country, and he was now the recognised king of one of the four great realms. Not bad for a freebooter who had landed a few years previously with ships and men but nothing else.

Anointed with chrism, holy oil, the new Christians were bound with white cloth where the oil touched. They would wear the white of new baptism for eight days, before the chrism-loosening. If Guthrum's baptism was an occasion to impress on the Vikings the spiritual awe of their new religion, the feast on the occasion of the chrism-loosening, and for a full twelve days afterwards, was a chance for the Anglo-Saxon hosts to impress on their guests the material and political advantages accruing to their new status. The ceremony of chrism-loosening took place at the nearby royal estate of Wedmore. Once the white cloths were undone, Guthrum and his men were feasted and sung in the manner only a king could. Furthermore, Alfred,

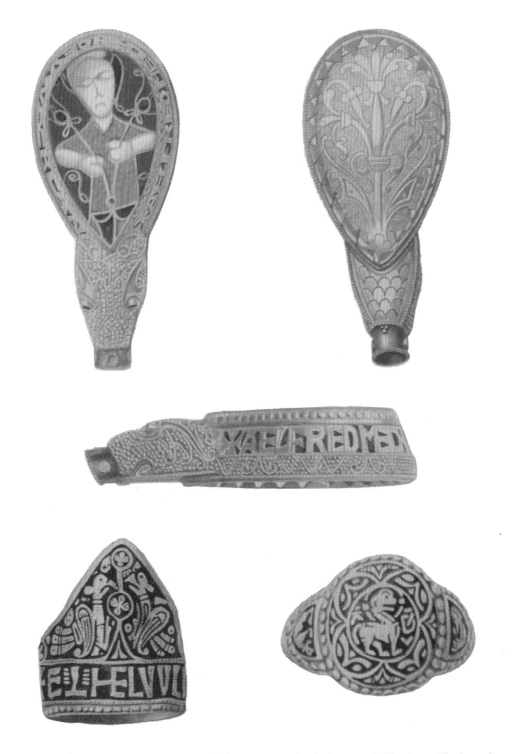

Top: 1. The Alfred Jewel, found near Athelney in 1693, back, front and side views. The legend round the side reads 'AELFRED MEC HEHT GEWYRCAN' – 'Alfred ordered me to be made'.

Bottom left: 2. The ring of King Æthelwulf, Alfred's father.

Bottom right: 3. The ring of Æthelswith, Alfred's sister.

RIST PÆSAEN NYDENINGAPUL

Opposite: 4. The statue of King Alfred in Wantage.

Above: 5. A page from the *Anglo-Saxon Chronicle*, thought to have been commissioned by Alfred.

Right: 6. A depiction of Alfred in a compilation of Anglo-Saxon, Norman and Angevin law codes.

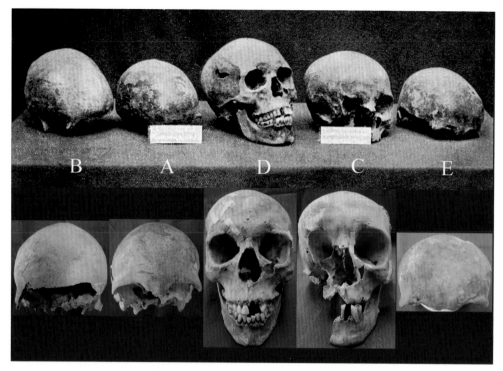

B A D C E

7. Photograph of the skulls found by John Mellor in 1866–7 and those excavated from the Unmarked Grave in 2013, demonstrating that they are the same.

8. The skulls in the grave.

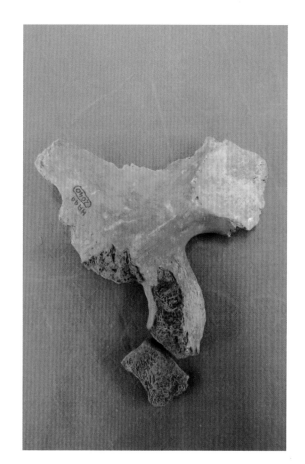

Right: 9. The pelvic bone discovered in 1999, thought to belong to Alfred the Great.

Below: 10. Looking into the Unmarked Grave.

12. The gravestone slab.

Opposite: 11. The bones in the Unmarked Grave prior to excavation.

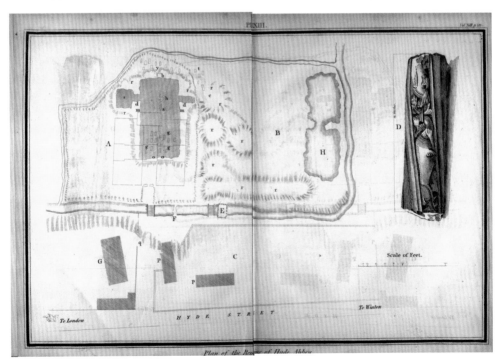

13. Plan of Hyde Abbey as revealed during the building works for the new Bridewell in 1788, with the location of the high altar at 'h' and the three stone coffins at 'a'. (From Howard 1800)

14. G. F. Watts' *Alfred Inciting the Saxons to Resist the Landing of the Danes*. Alfred is the central figure.

15. A depiction of a Viking ship from near the time of Alfred the Great. The image is from a picture stone in Stenkyrka, Gotland, Sweden.

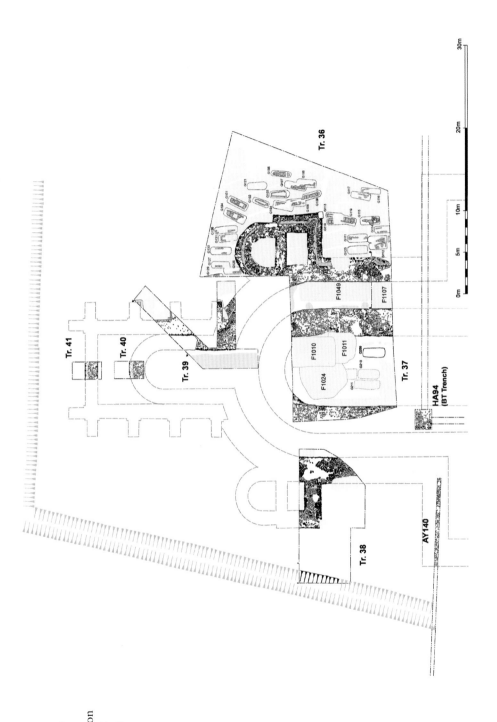

16. Plan of the 1990s excavations at Hyde Abbey, showing the location of the three pits at the east end of the church.

Tr. 36

Tr. 41

Tr. 40

Tr. 39

Tr. 37

Tr. 38

F1049

F1107

F1010

F1011

F1024

HA94
(BT Trench)

AY140

0m   5m   10m   20m   30m

17. Hyde Abbey Gatehouse as it appears today.

18. A stone capital from the original Hyde Abbey.

Opposite: 19. A ninth-century English sword, found in the Thames at Wallingford.

Above: 20. The Coronation Stone in Kingston upon Thames. Ælthelstan, Alfred's grandson, is believed to have been the first Anglo-Saxon king crowned here.

Left: 21. A portrait of Alfred from University College, Oxford.

22. A page from the *Anglo-Saxon Chronicle* detailing the Battle of Ashdown, at which Alfred commanded a division of the West Saxon army and was victorious against the Vikings.

23. *Alfred Rebuilding the Walls of London*, by F. O. Salisbury (1911).

24. The head of Alfred from a silver penny.

25. The Isle of Athelney, which was part of the Somerset swamps in Alfred's time. This is the area where, according to legend, he burnt the cakes before going to defeat the Vikings at the Battle of Edington.

DRYHTEN WÆS SPRECEN

ðas word ⁊ cwæð...

26. A manuscript page from Alfred's laws.

as king and ring giver, showered Guthrum and his men with the gold and silver fruits of their new status. Yes, they were subordinate to Alfred, but a great king was generous and they now benefited from his generosity. And if some among the Vikings had struggled to understand the significance of their earlier baptism, surely none failed to understand the message Alfred was conveying to them now: continued co-operation would bring further rewards, reneging on the deal would bring the vengeance of the new god they had sworn to follow.

It must have been an initially tense feast, as men who had been trying to kill each other only a short time before settled at the long tables to eat and drink together. For Guthrum, though, it must have been a relief. As he had followed Alfred into the marshes with his thirty chief men, the possibility that he was handing himself over to be treacherously slain must surely have occurred to him – particularly since, if the roles had been reversed, he would have had no compunction about killing Alfred and his magnates. But Alfred had kept his word, and as the former enemies sat at table, Guthrum as much as Alfred must have been congratulating himself on turning a near-hopeless situation around.

Æthelstan, *née* Guthrum, returned to Chippenham with his men. It took until October 878 for the Great Heathen Army to finally withdraw from Wessex, a delay that might have seemed ominous to Alfred. But Guthrum was to keep to his word. Later, kings Alfred and Æthelstan signed a formal treaty, recognising the limits of each other's realms and setting out regulations to minimise cross-border conflicts, but the outlines of the deal were presumably agreed during the days of talking and eating at Wareham.

This is the peace which King Alfred and King Guthrum and the councillors of all the English race and all the people who are in East Anglia have all agreed on and confirmed with oaths, for themselves and for their subjects, both for the living and for the unborn, who care to have God's favour or ours.

1. First concerning our boundaries: up the Thames and then up the Lea, and along the Lea to its source, and then in a straight line to Bedford, then up the Ouse to Watling Street.[5]

This deal was signed in 886, when Alfred had followed up his victory by taking London, but the main boundaries of what became the Danelaw were now in place.

In 878, as the Great Heathen Army finally left his realm, Alfred must have given thanks to God, in prayer and in church, for his deliverance and the deliverance of his people. But if he had been saved now, he may also have reflected that he had largely wasted the years of peace he had won after the earlier withdrawal of the Great Army. Watching Guthrum and his men march away, Alfred resolved he would not let the peace he had now won go to waste.

Through the next decade, King Alfred embarked on a complete programme for the spiritual, cultural, social and military renewal of his kingdom. When the Vikings returned, he would be ready for them.

8

Rebuilding

If Alfred ever entertained the thought that, with the defeat of Guthrum, he had overcome the Viking threat, he was disabused of that notion before the Great Army even left Chippenham. In 879, another Viking fleet, one that had been raising havoc in Francia before meeting defeat from the forces of Louis III and Carloman II on the Loire, sailed up the Thames and made fortified camp on the north shore of the river, at Fulham. They were on the Mercian side of the river, but nevertheless, Alfred certainly did not need another great army turning up on the borders of his realm. Fortunately for the king, it seems Guthrum was not too keen on more Vikings arriving either. Soon after the Fulham fleet arrived, the Great Army finally made good on its promise to leave Wessex and marched back east, heading for East Anglia, where, according to the *Chronicle*, the men of the army divided up the land among them. Æthelstan, *née* Guthrum, was king of East Anglia now and, as king, did not welcome an encampment of raiders anywhere near his borders. The Fulham Vikings, caught between Alfred to the west and Guthrum to the east, took the hint and re-embarked upon their ships, taking sail to Ghent.

The easy pickings that had fallen, almost without their asking, into Viking laps through the salad days of the mid-ninth century were getting harder to come by. In Francia, Charles the Bald had issued the Edict of Pistres in 864, creating a mobile cavalry, the genesis of centuries of French chivalry, and ordering the building or refurbishment of fortified bridges across the major rivers of his country. Although scholars are divided as to how many bridge forts were actually built, there did not need to be that many of them to gravely hamper the freedom of movement the Viking raiders had enjoyed previously.

Although we have little record of the dealings and communication between Alfred and the other Christian kings of Europe, this appears to be more a result of the vagaries of preservation rather than evidence that he was not in regular contact with kings such as Charles the Bald. The letters that have survived, including one to the Patriarch of Jerusalem, suggest a lively and far-ranging correspondence that stretched far beyond the narrow confines of Alfred's kingdom and, given the king's curiosity and the practical need to find ways to deal with the Vikings, it's almost certain that he would have learned of Charles's new strategy.

Although the Fulham Vikings left of their own accord, their arrival, and the near disaster he had suffered against Guthrum, demonstrated clearly to Alfred that he had much to do to secure his kingdom and his people. The months he had spent in relative isolation on and around Athelney had given him the chance to think deeply on his previous years as king, and to analyse his own failures then. Now that God had given him victory – and time – it was up to him to use it. The next decade would demonstrate the searching practical intelligence that Alfred brought to his understanding of the problem he, and Wessex, faced.

First, there was the why. Alfred approached his analysis of danger in a systematic way, working through the why, where, when and how of the Viking invasion. Any general might seek to understand where, when and how his enemy might attack, but for Alfred the fundamental question he needed to answer was why. Why had the Vikings attacked the Anglo-Saxon kingdoms? Or, to be more precise, why had they been permitted, by God, to attack and lay waste Northumbria, East Anglia, Mercia and, almost, Wessex? For we must remember that Alfred did not believe in a random universe, where things happened by chance, nor in one where the fate singers weaved destinies through their inscrutable whim, but one in which events, through God's providence, were formed to produce certain ends, namely the growth of the faith Alfred professed and the felicity, in this life and the next, of men and women. The Christian message, when translated into an Anglo-Saxon cultural context, saw Jesus as 'liege lord of the heavens',[1] a king who came into the world to defeat, in personal combat, the lord of this world. The most sustained meditation on the nature of Jesus within an Old English context is 'The Dream of the Rood', a poem in which, using the traditional Anglo-Saxon riddling motifs, the narrator first has a vision of Christ's cross, and then the Cross itself speaks of its experience.

> Then I saw, marching toward me,
> mankind's brave King;
>   He came to climb upon me …
>
> Almighty God ungirded Him,
>   eager to mount the gallows,
> Unafraid in the sight of many:
>   he would set free mankind.
> I shook when His arms embraced me
>   but I durst not bow to the ground,
> stoop to the Earth's surface.
>   Stand fast I must.[2]

Such a God did not allow a pagan people to ravage His own without reason, and Alfred naturally first sought that reason within the Bible. There, through the long and tortured history of the descendants of Abraham, one theme resounded: when the people of God turned away from their lord, then God would send first messengers, then scourges, to bring them back again. The great genius of the Jews, and the seed of their survival as a people when pretty well every other displaced people in history disappeared once removed from their homeland, was to understand their travails at the hands of contemporary superpowers as the workings out of their own relationship with God, rather than the workings out of the politics of their time. Thus, when the Babylonians conquered Jerusalem, destroying the Temple and deporting the leading Jews to their capital, the prophet Jeremiah understood this all to be a consequence of the Jews' own behaviour. 'And when the people ask, "Why has the LORD our God done all this to us?" you will tell them, "As you have forsaken me and served foreign gods in your own land, so now you will serve foreigners in a land not your own"' (Jeremiah 5:19).

The analogy was made all the more apt for Alfred in that his own people were Christians, and thus chosen by God as were the Jews in the Bible, but the invaders – be they Babylonians or Vikings – were in both cases pagans. Thus he could clearly argue that God would use a pagan people to chastise his own. With that established in his own mind, Alfred had to understand what he and his people had done to break their covenant with God and call down such a punishment upon themselves.

In his *Ecclesiastical History of the English People*, along with pretty much inventing the idea of an English people, Bede also warns against a creeping laxity that, he feared, was beginning to take root among the clergy of his time, and compares that to the earlier devotion of the first apostles to the English. But Bede had died in 735, a century and a half before, and Alfred, presumably from his personal knowledge and through the testimony of his bishops, did not follow Bede's belief in a general laxity of the English Church, although such a diagnosis, moral falling away requiring a return to spiritual first principles, has been a recurring theme of Judaism and Christianity, from Elijah, the 'troubler of Israel' (1 Kings 18:17), railing against the worship of Baal, to Martin Luther exposing papal abuses. It would have been natural – and complete with Biblical precedent – for Alfred to have ascribed the problems of his kingdom to a failure of his clergy to follow their religion properly.

Only, he did not do this. For Alfred, the clear cause of the punishment God laid upon his English people was not so much a lapse in religion in general, but a failure to inculcate learning in England, particularly in comparison to a previous golden age of scholarship in the seventh century, when men like Bede and Alcuin were the foremost scholars in Europe, which Alfred believed to be responsible for a golden age of peace and prosperity in the country.

Uniquely, we have Alfred's own words to describe what once was the state of England, and what he hoped to restore:

I would have it known that very often it has come to my mind what men of learning there were formerly throughout England, both in religious and secular orders; and how there were happy times then throughout England; and how the kings, who had authority over the people, obeyed God and his messengers; and how they not only maintained peace, morality and authority at home but also extended their territory outside; and how they succeeded both in warfare and in wisdom; and also how eager were the religious orders both in teaching and in learning as well as in all the holy services which it was their duty to perform for God; and how people from abroad sought wisdom and instruction in this country; and how nowadays, if we wished to acquire these things, we would have to seek them outside. Learning had declined so thoroughly in England that there were very few men on this side of the Humber who could understand their divine services in English, or even translate a single letter from Latin into English; and I suppose that there were not many beyond the Humber either. There were so few of them that I cannot recollect even a single one south of the

Thames when I succeeded to the kingdom. Thanks be to God Almighty that we now have any supply of teachers at all! Therefore I beseech you to do as I believe you *are* willing to do: as often as you can, free yourself from worldly affairs so that you may apply that wisdom which God gave you wherever you can. Remember what punishments befell us in this world when we ourselves did not cherish learning nor transmit it to other men. We were Christians in name alone, and very few of us possessed Christian virtues.[3]

So, while the virtues had lapsed, as virtues are wont to do, Alfred was in no doubt that the key reason for the punishments that had fallen upon his kingdom, and the other Anglo-Saxon kingdoms, was the failure to cherish learning. It was, in many ways, an extraordinary conclusion, and one that appears to be without precedent or, indeed, 'succeedent'. While there certainly seems to have been a falling away, particularly in Latin literacy, in the ninth century, this appears to be as much a result of the Viking invasions as a cause – even a spiritual cause – to them. The Viking attacks on Kent appear to have had a devastating effect on the metropolitan see at Canterbury, with the surviving charters from the cathedral showing a precipitous decline in the quality, indeed in the most basic understanding, of Latin, until a nadir is reached in 873, with a document that is so poorly written as to be all but incomprehensible:

When solemn Latin diplomas had to be written either by a man who could no longer see to write or by a man who knew little or no Latin, then it is clear that the metropolitan church must have been quite unable to provide any effective training in the scriptures or in Christian worship.[4]

So, it is clear that learning had declined through most of England, but how many warrior kings of the early medieval period would have ascribed their enemies' success to a lack of trained Latinists? Only one: Alfred. By that very diagnosis, Alfred gives us a unique window into the twin chambers of his soul, for he was as much a scholar as a warrior, a man who was at home poring over a translation from Latin into English as standing at the centre of the shield wall. It is this duality to his nature, but a duality that Alfred always sought to bring to a creative synthesis, that marks Alfred as exceptional among rulers. Having identified learning as lost, he set about restoring it. To that end, he applied the same methods as a king employed to attract warriors to his court: gold and glory, but given to clerics rather than the psychopathic peacock that was the Anglo-Saxon warrior.

Later in the passage quoted above, Alfred names four clerics who were engaged in helping him to revive learning: Plegemund, Asser, John and Grimbald. Of these, Plegemund was a Mercian and Asser (who became Alfred's biographer) was Welsh. But in his search for learned men, Alfred was perfectly willing to recruit beyond the shores of Britain: John was from Saxony and Grimbald from Thérouanne, thirty miles east of Boulogne. The renewal of English knowledge was to be an international affair.

But first, Alfred had to renew learning in himself. According to Asser – and this he must have learned from the king first hand – Alfred was deeply abashed by the fact that he did not learn to read and write English until he was twelve. English, though, was only a first stage; Latin was the language of learning and of God, and sometime around 887 Alfred, now nearing forty, set himself to the task of learning the language for himself, and to a sufficient standard that he might be able to take on the task of translating Latin texts into English. Asser, who comes close to breaking the first commandment against idolatry in his veneration for Alfred, reports that the king 'began through divine inspiration to read [Latin] and to translate it at the same time, all on one and the same day'.[5] As Alfred had assembled his group of cleric scholars, and worked hard with them, the day Asser had in mind might be one when various elements clicked together in Alfred's mind, allowing him to see through the externals of a language to its heart, and go from there.

Since Asser first came to Alfred's notice in 886, and became a member of his establishment a year later, we know that it was only later on in the 880s that Alfred mastered Latin. His programme of cultural renewal had begun at the beginning of the decade, however. The first step had been the recruitment of Mercian clerics. Alfred's victory over Guthrum had allowed him to expand his influence into western Mercia, and the courting of clerics had the additional benefit of smoothing the way for Alfred to be accepted as overking of Mercia. Bishops were magnates in their own right, lords of large estates, with retinues of armed retainers as well as clerks. They also provided a useful counterbalance against the power and ambition of secular magnates, while providing the king with the trained and literate staff that Alfred had determined were necessary for the functioning of his kingdom.

From Mercia, along with Plegemund, Alfred also brought into his entourage Werferth, the bishop of Worcester. A reasonable number of charters survive with Werferth's name upon them, allowing us to say more about this bishop than most other ninth-century churchmen. Taking the name stem Wer- as a sign of family relationship (think of Alfred's brothers and sister, all christened names beginning with Æthel-), then Werferth was a scion of a noble family with strong ecclesiastical connections and representation in Kent – for instance, there were two bishops of Rochester called Wermund. Werferth was born around 830, probably to Werenberht, an ealdorman of Mercia who appeared as a witness in charters from 845 to 855, rising to third place in the strictly hierarchical list during those ten years. Werenberht was doing well, and that allowed for advancement for his son, Werferth, particularly with two further members of the family, Wernod and Werhard, being abbots of St Augustine's, Canterbury, and Christ Church, Canterbury, respectively. With the metropolitan see of Canterbury being the primatial bishopric in the country, the young Werferth was in the right place to enter holy orders and begin an ecclesiastical career.

Werferth was a talented young man, and as Kent had become part of the kingdom of Wessex he was soon seconded to the royal circle, appearing as witness in charters from the reign of King Æthelwulf, Alfred's father. Fascinatingly, Werferth's name always appears in these lists very close to those of Æthelwulf's youngest sons, Æthelred and Alfred, and just after the two princes a thegn called Esne is named. A charter was witnessed when a document, its contents having been agreed on by an assembly, was placed on the altar and, working around the room in order of seniority, the men present came forward to lay their hands upon the document and give oath to its truth. Thus, in the assembly, the young Abbot Werferth must have been standing beside the æthelings Æthelred and Alfred, with Esne on their other side. From this, we can hazard that Werferth and Esne had charge of Æthelred and Alfred, perhaps as tutor and governor respectively. That Alfred accorded Werferth particular respect and gratitude through his life is shown by the king leaving him, by name, 100 mancuses (one mancus was equivalent to one gold coin or thirty silver pennies) in his will – a considerable amount and the same as he left his ealdormen. In that will, Alfred also left 100 mancuses to a Bishop Esne, raising the thought that the thegn who had guarded the young æthelings may have taken vows and entered holy orders, while remaining in the favour of his king and old friend.

Werferth does not appear in the meagre records for the 860s, but was consecrated bishop of Worcester on 7 June 873, having been appointed bishop the year before. Worcester was a Mercian diocese, so for Werferth to have been appointed to it by King Burgred he would have had to have been released by Wessex. In 873, Alfred had, just about, survived the first great Viking assault on his kingdom and was trying to shore up support and allies. Having his old tutor and friend made bishop of Worcester helped to further cement the tie between Wessex and Mercia that had been created by his sister marrying King Burgred. Of course, events would force Burgred and Æthelswith to flee their kingdom, but Werferth proved a consummate survivor, remaining bishop of Worcester for forty-two years.

The surviving charters let us see something of Werferth's activities as bishop, which included being present as witness and adviser when Alfred visited Mercia, organising towns, leasing the estates of churches, both his own and others within the diocese, court cases involving his estates, and buying and selling land. In the ninth century land was money, and a bishop had a lot of it. But that money went towards many ends, including the support of the bishop's staff. Various charters list Werferth's priests and retainers, showing that he employed more than fifty men fit to witness legal documents, split roughly two to three in favour of secular followers over clerical ones. Many of these men probably had their own retainers, whether they be clerks, servants or assistants in the case of the priests, and fighting men and grooms for the laymen.

Tallying this up, we find that, when Bishop Werferth travelled through his diocese, it would have been in the midst of a considerable caravan: some twenty or thirty priests and clerks, an armed escort of maybe a hundred men, and then as many servants, grooms and carters. Learning this, one begins to understand why so many early medieval holy men and monks strove mightily to avoid being made bishop – for anyone who wished to devote their time to God and prayer, the responsibilities of a bishop must have seemed vexing indeed. Of course, the evidence of charters gives us an insight into a bishop's worldly responsibilities, showing how many there were, but his chief role lay in leading worship at his cathedral church – given the length of early medieval services, a bishop was not a man with much spare time on his hands.

Nevertheless, Alfred required Werferth to join in his efforts to achieve a cultural renewal, and gave to him the task of translating into Old English Pope Gregory the Great's *Dialogues*, written as a dialogue – naturally – between Gregory and his friend, Peter, a deacon, where Peter bemoans the fact that their native land, Italy, lacks the notable hermit saints of Egypt and the surrounding desert. Gregory puts Peter right by telling him of the many extraordinary Italian saints. It's a book full of miracles and signs, not normally to the taste of modern readers, but it opened up a world of wonders to Alfred and his bishops, and provided a great impetus to the knowledge of St Benedict, the founder of western monasticism and the subject of a quarter of the book. It also dealt with the immortality of the soul. As a man who had seen death at the closest of quarters, it was a vital question for Alfred. The old religion of the Anglo-Saxons seems to have accorded little thought to an afterlife, beyond the roistering of warriors who died in battle. For the rest, death seems to have meant not an end, but an existence as an insubstantial shade, akin to the bloodless ghosts of Hades. Alfred had seen the light go from men's eyes, he had lost children himself and ordered the execution of prisoners and criminals. For a man with his restless intellect, the question of what happened to people after death was something he wrestled with throughout his life. Gregory's *Dialogues* were part of the answer. The Anglo-Saxons also revered Pope Gregory as their apostle, for he had sent the mission of St Augustine to Canterbury in AD 596, and this may have further influenced Alfred to have this work translated. Emphasising the importance he attached to it, Alfred wrote a short preface to the book and then had it sent out to the bishops of the land, commending the work for the solace it brought the mind amid the tribulations of life.

The king commissioned two other translations into Old English: *Histories Against the Pagans* (*Historiae adversus Paganos*) by Paulus Orosius and Bede's *Ecclesiastical History of the English People*. Orosius wrote in the fifth century, at the behest of his friend St Augustine of Hippo, telling, basically, the history of the world. The translator, adopting a fairly free approach, adds and alters the source text to make it more relevant to a ninth-century readership, bringing out clearly a message that history is a story written by God's hand – a message that Alfred, as agent of God's will, wanted to bring home to his bishops and magnates. They were all actors in God's great drama, their parts depending on their fealty to the king who had been anointed by God at this time of trial. Orosius's history of the world provided a companion history to Bede's history of the English people. One or more of the many Mercian clerics in Alfred's circle may have been the first to draw out the implications for their own time of Bede's idea of an English people, united by worship of one God rather than divided by their antecedents being Angle or Saxon, when Alfred, king of the West Saxons, was in the process of becoming overking of the Anglian Mercians – two kingdoms that had long been rivals. With a common pagan enemy, Alfred as king of the one English people, rather than monarch of just the West Saxons, began to make sense to his Mercian clergy. And, although Alfred continued to be styled king of the West Saxons through to the end of his reign, on coins and charters and in the treaty signed with Guthrum, he began to adopt different titles alluding to the concept towards which he and his court were groping: king of the English people.

Not content with commissioning translations, Alfred himself undertook to 'turn into the language that we can all understand certain books which are the most necessary for all men to know',[6] namely Pope Gregory the Great's *Pastoral Care*, *The Consolation of Philosophy* by Anicius Boethius, the *Soliloquies* of St Augustine and the first fifty Psalms from the Bible. Alfred also wrote a long preface to the translation of Gregory's *Pastoral Care*, some of which is quoted above, explaining to his readers the purpose behind the books he was sending out to his bishops and people. The process of translation was probably collaborative, with Alfred and his scholar priests reading out the text and discussing the meaning before the king dictated to an amanuensis the agreed translation. Indeed, in the preface to *Pastoral Care*, Alfred specified that he translated 'sometimes word for word, sometimes sense for sense'.[7] These occasions, where the king departed from a literal translation, provide us with a particular insight into the mind of the man and the concerns that were most important to him.

But, more than anything else, what Alfred chose to translate indicates his chief concerns. Gregory's *Pastoral Care* was, essentially, a manual for bishops, but in its advice for dealing with the problems of high office its message was one that Alfred could both identify with personally and commend to the attention of his secular magnates. For the book describes the qualities necessary in a man to be a soul shepherd, and Alfred, as king, saw himself as responsible for the spiritual wellbeing of his people as well as their physical security. Where

Gregory emphasised the necessity for bishops to continually examine and reflect upon their consciences, the chastened, post Chippenham Alfred, could parse this both as a call to personal repentance but also as a summons to re-examining the way he ruled his kingdom. And where Gregory states that learning is a requirement for rulers, Alfred found the pope that his people revered most stating one of the fundamental beliefs of his own heart. The pope, who had experienced vicissitudes himself, also counsels on how troubles prune the soul and thus, after the initial pain, make it healthier, as well as the necessity for bishops to remain firm in the face of the distractions of the world; a useful admonition for a man as busy as Bishop Werferth, and even more so for a king.

Alfred was shrewd enough to guess that Gregory's pastoral advice might best be gold-plated with an earthly gift:

> I intend to send a copy to each bishopric in my kingdom; and in each copy there will be an *æstel* worth fifty mancuses.[8]

(An *æstel* was probably a book marker; many scholars believe the exquisite Alfred Jewel, now kept in the Ashmolean Museum, which has the inscription '+ AELFRED MEC HEHT GEWRYRCAN' ('Alfred ordered me to be made') on its side, was an *æstel*, with a pointer to keep place when reading fitting in the empty socket at its end. The Alfred jewel is itself a salutary reminder of the wealth and technical expertise that was available to the king in ninth-century Wessex, and makes the determined efforts of the Vikings to conquer the kingdom more understandable. After all, if such a jewel could be handed out as a gift to each bishopric in Wessex and Mercia, then there must have been considerable wealth in Britain at the time.)

With Pope Gregory's *Pastoral Care*, Alfred and his advisers stuck close to the literal sense of the words, but with his next two translations Alfred allowed himself considerably more latitude, interpolating and occasionally even rewriting the texts to make them more relevant to an Anglo-Saxon readership and to reflect his own considered thought on the subject. *The Consolation of Philosophy* is a meditation on providence and its acceptance, written by a Roman, Boethius, of late antiquity who had reached high office under the Emperor Theodoric but was accused of treachery and arrested. Boethius wrote the *Consolation* while under arrest – one hopes it spoke for his soul too, as providence decreed that there would be no reprieve for him: Boethius was executed. Although Boethius was Christian, the book is written as a dialogue between him and Lady Philosophy, and it comes from a world which valued its classical heritage as well as its new Christian faith. Alfred must have found its treatment of fortitude in the face of affliction inspiring in view of his own experiences, but he recasts the book, changing the conversation into one between Mind and Reason, and rewriting many of the classical allusions that would have meant little to a ninth-century Anglo-Saxon readership into more familiar, concrete forms. It is this translation that includes Alfred's own thoughts – not found in the original – of his reluctance to become king as well as the tools a king must use:

Look, Wisdom, you know that desire for and possession of earthly power never pleased me overmuch, and that I did not unduly desire this earthly rule, but that nevertheless I wished for tools and resources for the task that I was commanded to accomplish, which was that I should virtuously and worthily guide and direct the authority which was entrusted to me ... In the case of the king, the resources and tools with which to rule are that he have his land fully manned: he must have praying men, fighting men and working men ... Another aspect of his resources is that he must have the means of support for his tools, the three classes of men. These, then, are their means of support: land to live on, gifts, weapons, food, ale, clothing, and whatever else is necessary for the three classes of men.[9]

It is a telling passage: Alfred has taken a text steeped in neo-Platonism and, viewing it with a practical intelligence grounded in the exigencies of running and defending a kingdom, turned it into a short manual on kingship. This was characteristic of the king. Where he had to substitute his own analogies for obscure ones in the book he was translating, he used images and activities that were well known to his people, from a man using the land leased to him by his lord for hunting, fowling and fishing, through to a housebuilder cutting timber in the forest for the homes he is building.

St Augustine's *Soliloquies* is probably the most unexpected among Alfred's choices of books 'most necessary for all men to know'.[10] Not that Augustine was an unusual addition to the canon of knowledge – the African bishop has remained a dominant influence on the Church through the centuries, so much so that, a millennium and a half after his death, he and Thomas Aquinas were the two most cited authors in the *Catechism of the Catholic Church* – but when faced with the chance of translating works such as *City of God*, *Confessions* and *On The Trinity*, picking his *Soliloquies* was unusual. But the subject matter makes clear why Alfred chose this particular work. Augustine wrote *Soliloquies* as a dialogue between himself and his reason on the question of the immortality of the soul, reason leading him to an appreciation of its eternal nature and destiny. The nature and immortality or otherwise of the soul was an abiding concern of the king, in which one must surely see the imaginative conscience of a man who has seen, and dealt out, a great deal of dying.

> There is no doubt that souls are immortal. Believe your own reason, and believe Christ the Son of God, and believe all His saints, because they were very reliable witnesses, and believe your own soul, which through its own reason tells you continually that it is within you. It likewise tells you that it is eternal, because it strives after eternal things. It is not so foolish a creature as to seek what it cannot find, nor to strive after what it cannot possess or what does not belong to it. Abandon now your unjustifiable doubt: it is sufficiently clear that you are eternal and shall exist forever.[11]

The final translation that we can attribute to Alfred is, unlike the *Soliloquies*, not in the least surprising as a book 'most necessary for all men to know': the Psalms. Alfred translated the first fifty Psalms of the Bible – William of Malmesbury, writing in the twelfth century, said that the king was working on the translation when he died, hence only the first fifty were completed.

The Psalms, since the earliest days of Christianity, provided the language of daily prayer for the Church. According to tradition, they were mainly composed by David, songs and laments and exultations to His Lord, the dialogue of a soul with its Maker, moving from the depths of despair when a radical clinging to trust in God when all seems lost is all that is left to a David, in exile and hunted, through to praise hymns of triumph as his enemies are delivered into his hands and he is justified in the eyes of his people. Generations upon generations have found solace, inspiration and courage in the Psalms; for Alfred, they were a virtual biography, and translating them must have been as much an act of worship and thanksgiving as of education.

The king introduced each Psalm with a short preface, giving a background and gloss to the text, and again giving us a privileged window into his mind; read Alfred's translation of the second Psalm: is it not the king, himself, taking David's prayer as his own?

> The text of the following psalm is called psalmus David, that is, 'David's Psalm' in English. It is so called because David in this psalm lamented and complained to the Lord about his enemies, both native and foreign, and about all his troubles. And everyone who sings this psalm does likewise with respect to his own enemies ...

> 7. For the Lord said to me: 'You are my son – I begot you this very day.
> 8. Ask me, and I shall deliver the enemy peoples for your inheritance, and I shall extend your authority over their boundaries.
> 9. And I shall bring it about that you rule them with an iron

rod; and I can destroy them as easily as the potter can a pot.'

10. Hear now, you kings, and learn, you judges who judge over the earth:

11. Serve the Lord and fear Him; rejoice in God, yet with awe.

12. Embrace learning, lest you incur God's anger and lest you stray from the right path.

13. For when His anger is kindled, then blessed are those who now trust in Him.

These translations and writings are unique among kings of the period, and not exactly commonplace among monarchs of any era. Two scholars have argued, forcefully, that the biography of Alfred by Asser is a forgery, but even if that were the case – and I and most historians do not believe it to be so – these works by Alfred would still tell us more about his mind and heart than we know of any other king of the time.

But Alfred was a king. These were not private devotions, but his prescription for his kingdom as much as his own soul. The king had learned to read and write Latin as a mature man; if he could do so, then the very least his magnates, officials and reeves could do was learn to read and write in their native tongue. If they were to retain their office, this motley crew of grizzled warriors had to apply themselves to their letters. Hands more used to wielding swords found themselves wrung out from cramp as, hunched over slates, Alfred's magnates painstakingly learned their ABCs. It is a thoroughly entertaining image, made more so when Asser adds that if the magnate was too old or set in his ways to learn himself, then the king commanded that someone, be it son, relative, freeman or slave, be on hand to read aloud from the books 'most necessary to know' day and night.

To inculcate a love of learning in his own children, and the children of his nobility, Alfred set up what was, in effect, a court school. Its establishment had to wait upon the more settled conditions obtained after the victory at the Battle of Edington in 878, so Alfred's firstborn children, his daughter Æthelflæd and son Edward, missed out on the court school, although tutors had given these two their letters at least. Æthelflæd had married when the court school was established, but Edward, a young prince and already a battlefield commander, attended lessons alongside his younger siblings: one suspects that Alfred's view on the worthiness of his son to succeed him would have been as influenced by Edward's proclivities in the classroom as his exploits on the battlefield. The court school also taught the children of noblemen, and 'a good many of lesser birth as well'[12] how to read in Latin and English – it would be too much to say that Alfred intended universal literacy, but his solution to the problem of the loss of learning and its consequences was characteristically original. Two generations earlier, Charlemagne had embarked on something similar with the scholars he had imported – most notably from Northumbria – but where the first Holy Roman Emperor set out to improve the knowledge of Latin in his realm, Alfred, looking at the situation of his kingdom and the already widespread use of the vernacular, had both English and Latin taught to clerics and laity.

In order to achieve this programme, Alfred needed scholars. At the time, the only scholars were clergy – the Church and learning were completely intertwined. As Alfred consolidated his influence in Mercia in the years after the Battle of Edington, it was relatively straightforward for him to bring Mercian clerics, such as Æthelstan, Werwulf and Plegemund, later archbishop of Canterbury, into his court. Despite the long rivalry and division between the two kingdoms, the Mercian clergy became among the most fervent supporters of Alfred's supremacy. This served the king well, allowing him to smooth over his subjugation of a kingdom that once aspired to mastery over Wessex. Alfred was the only king left to the Anglo-Saxons, he fervently supported learning, was intensely religious and, if the Mercian clerics had any remaining doubts, Alfred 'showered them with many honours and entitlements in the kingdom of the West Saxons'[13]. It did not take any great insight to see where their future best lay.

But for his programme to succeed, Alfred needed more men, so he spread his search farther. Around 885, Alfred invited the Welsh bishop of St David's to join his court. This bishop was Asser, the author of Alfred's biography, and a shadowy and disputed figure among scholars. But let us assume his truth for the moment, and see what he says of his coming to Alfred's attention.

Wales was the land of the Britons, the original inhabitants of the country. The Anglo-Saxons had gradually expanded their control over the centuries, pushing the ruling elite westwards. (Whether this expansion was accompanied by some form of ethnic cleansing, and a wholesale exchange of populations, or was rather the conquering of one ruling elite by another, and the gradual assimilation of the general population to the culture of the rulers, remains a subject of debate. A telling point of the

Anglo-Saxon attitude to the Britons is that the word 'Welsh' derives from *wealh* – slave.) In the ninth century, Wales was split into eight kingdoms, the princes of which fought with each other as much as with the neighbouring Anglo-Saxons. Asser first came to Alfred to ask his protection and alliance, as the foremost king in the land, against the king who ruled Dyfed, the principality where his monastery, St David's, was located in the far west of modern-day Pembrokeshire. After travelling 'across a great expanse of land',[14] Asser tells of his first meeting with the king:

> I arrived in the territory of the right-hand [southern] Saxons, which in English is called Sussex, accompanied by some English guides. There I saw him for the first time at the royal estate which is called Dean. When I had been warmly welcomed by him, and we were engaged in discussion, he asked me earnestly to commit myself to his service and to become a member of his household.[15]

Alfred, naturally, offered gifts too, but Asser answered that he had to consult with the members of his community first. Then Alfred suggested an arrangement whereby Asser split his time equally between St David's and Wessex, spending six months in each. The Welshman promised to return in six months' time to Wessex with his reply but, on his journey home, he contracted an illness which left him convalescing for a year at the monastery in Caerwent (in modern-day Monmouthshire). When the illness finally abated, Asser returned to St David's and received the blessing of his community for a life of timesharing; for the monks of St David's, having Alfred as patron meant powerful protection against the interference of the king of Dyfed, who was wont to get involved in matters the monks regarded as purely ecclesiastical, expelling the bishop, including Asser on one occasion. For Asser, engagement at King Alfred's court brought him, and the carefully hoarded learning of the Welsh which had survived centuries of endemic warfare with the (originally pagan) Anglo-Saxons, into contact and fruitful exchange with a national and international group of scholars. It also brought Asser a great many gifts: monasteries in Congresbury and Banwell and their associated benefices, 'an extremely valuable silk cloak and a quantity of incense weighing as much as a stout man',[16] and, ultimately, the bishopric of Sherborne. It was a good deal for the Welshman, but anyone reading his life of Alfred can see there that Asser's admiration for the king was unfeigned: he genuinely loved the man – indeed, rather too much for the taste of a historian; Asser allows little in the way of shadows to intrude into his portrait of his beloved lord. This may have been for quite practical reasons as well; the intended audience was likely the clergy of the kingdoms of Wales, still doubtful about accepting an Anglo-Saxon – their enemy of old – as overking.

Not content with having scoured Britain for scholars, Alfred also turned his attention abroad. John the Old Saxon was not aged, but rather from 'Old' Saxony as opposed to being an Anglo-Saxon. We do not know how he came to Alfred's attention, but from about 885 he was part of Alfred's circle of ecclesiastical scholars and counsellors. Alfred must have held him in high esteem indeed, because he made John abbot of one of only two monasteries he founded, and the one set at the most fateful location of the king's life: Athelney.

John's tenure as abbot of Athelney proved somewhat more colourful than Alfred, or indeed John, would have wished. As a newly established house in an unprepossessing location, Alfred had to import monks and servants to man the monastery from abroad. Among them were a Gallic priest and deacon who, for reasons Asser does not divulge, took such a dislike of their abbot, John, that they hatched a plot to murder him. They bribed two Gallic slaves to slip into the abbey church in the night and wait there, under cover, for John. The abbot had the habit of going each night into the church to pray alone, and the assassins were to murder him as he prayed before the altar and then drag the body from the monastery and dump it outside the door of a well-known local prostitute, thus ensuring posthumous libel as well as death. Sure enough, John came into the church to pray but when the would-be murderers attacked him, they found, to their consternation, that the abbot had once been a warrior. Although unarmed, John managed to fend off the attackers long enough for his shouts to raise the community and, although wounded, the abbot survived. The attackers escaped, but were tracked down and caught. Under rather brutal questioning they told their story, so the priest and deacon were apprehended as well, and all four 'underwent a terrible death through various tortures'.[17] Asser's short comment is almost enough to make one feel sorry for them.

Apart from John the Old Saxon, Alfred also recruited a Frank, named Grimbald. Grimbald was a priest and monk at the abbey of St Bertin at St Omer, and Alfred had to work hard to get permission from Grimbald's bishop for him to come to

Wessex. Although we don't have the text of Alfred's letter to Archbishop Fulco of Rheims, we have Fulco's reply. From that, we know that, to sweeten the deal, Alfred sent with his request some fine dogs – the hounds of Britain had been a valuable, high-status export since the days of the Roman Empire, and they continued to be throughout the early medieval period. Little else seemed to impress Fulco about the people into whose hands he was, somewhat gingerly, entrusting a monk whom he had marked for high office in Francia. In the course of his letter to the king, the archbishop mentioned, in a passing but slighting fashion, that 'the educating of barbaric savagery' required easy baby steps before 'an uncultivated and barbarous people'[18] would be able to fulfil the precepts of the Church. To that end, he was willing, although reluctant, to send Grimbald, on the understanding that Grimbald would be given the same high office in Wessex that he was to have received in Francia.

The assurances Alfred gave must have satisfied Fulco, for he sent Grimbald to Britain, but the monk never held high ecclesiastical office – the king refers to him as his 'mass-priest', and his 'mass-priest' he remained. Later tradition states that Grimbald's own humility stood in the way of his advancement: when the see of Canterbury fell vacant and was offered to him, Grimbald dodged the ecclesiastical bullet and recommended the Mercian Plegemund instead.

Apart from these scholars, Alfred maintained an open court, welcoming travellers and merchants and scholars with tales to tell of distant lands. Amid its tales of battles and wars, the *Chronicle* tells of the unexpected arrival of three visitors at Alfred's court in 891:

And three Irishmen came to King Alfred in a boat without any oars from Ireland, whence they had stolen away because they wished to go on pilgrimage for the love of God, they cared not where. The boat from which they travelled was made from two and a half hides; and they took with them only enough food for seven days. And after seven days they came to land in Cornwall, and then went immediately to King Alfred. Their names were Dubslaine, Macbethath, and Maelinmuin.[19]

Irish monks, reading accounts of early Christian anchorites, hungered for the desert and its privations, but were trapped in a country in which death by drowning was rather more of a prospect than dying of thirst.

The *Cambrai Homily*, the earliest known Irish sermon, dating from the seventh or early eighth century, reveals quite precisely how these monks at the world's end understood their calling:

> Precious in the eyes of God:
> The white martyrdom of exile
> The green martyrdom of the hermit
> The red martyrdom of sacrifice.

In response, there grew among them the practice of pilgrimage, of putting all one's trust in God, all one's goods into a coracle, and casting off upon the face of the deep. No doubt many such pilgrims soon met a watery end, but others drifted far, fetching up all over the place. And the place where they landed they saw as God's provision for them, the place, if it was sufficiently remote and windswept, to make their hermitage and their peace with God. Alfred's court probably was not sufficiently remote, so in all likelihood his Irish visitors moved on, leaving the Chronicler to marvel at their coming.

Alfred was a general who lost many battles but ultimately won the war. He was a warlord, capable of leading men hard schooled in bloodshed, and keeping them faithful to him. He was a ring giver and generous lord. But, really, these were the minimum requirements for a king who would reign for any length of time during this era. It is Alfred's devotion to and fostering of learning that sets him apart from his fellows. All early medieval kings were acutely conscious of their image, for glory was the best advertising for a king: it deterred enemies and attracted followers. Every king had a scop, a court poet, whose job it was to cast praise poems, in the alliterative meter of Anglo-Saxon verse, extolling the virtues and victories of their royal patron, and keeping the collective memory of the court. Alfred loved the vernacular poems and songs of his people, so he surely would have had a scop, strumming the six-string Anglo-Saxon lyre and declaiming the victory at Ashdown and, even more dramatically, the flight from Chippenham into the marshes and the victory at Edington. All kings of the time, Anglo-Saxon and Viking and Pict and Irish, had such poets in their retinues. But Alfred was unique in his devotion to the written word too. He was as careful to shape his name in the words on the page as he was in forming the words chanted into the hall. To that end, Alfred commissioned the compilation of the *Anglo-Saxon Chronicle*. This tale of years, with its bald statements of battles and deaths, is a crucial historical document but, as such, must be viewed carefully. The history of the time before his reign was patched together from a variety of sources, notably Bede and a variety of existing chronicles detailing the histories of Mercian, Kentish, South Saxon and West Saxon kingdoms, and after its compilation copies were dispatched through the land which then formed the basis for ongoing chronicling. There are eight extant manuscripts, each different, and the disentangling of sources, influences and histories is an ongoing scholarly pursuit. Although there is little comment in the Alfredian portion of the *Chronicle*, the choice and, in particular, the omissions were part of the image Alfred and his circle wanted to project of a West Saxon king as the culmination of Anglo-Saxon history and the bulwark against pagan invaders. Still, where it has been possible to check the *Chronicle* independently it has proved a reliable historical guide, so the previous notion that it is pure Alfredian propaganda has been quietly put to one side. It would be better regarded as an honest record, but one informed and formed by its point of view and time of composition. The Viking threat, Alfred and his circle knew, was not over. They had won a remission, and they had used it, but there was no doubt among them that someday they would see the dragon ships' sails upon the horizon again.

9

Landhold

The king was a scholar, but he was not going to be a gentle man when the Vikings returned. Alfred had examined the problem and determined that the ultimate cause for the Viking attacks was the abandonment of learning – and thus the slackening of faith – among the Anglo-Saxons, and he had prescribed the solution: the translation and education programme he and his ecclesiastical scholars had embarked upon, and the learning he forced upon his magnates and officials on pain of losing their office. But although Alfred firmly believed that this would ultimately bring salvation to his people, he knew well enough that it was a long-term project, and in the meantime there were marauding Viking armies who would, sooner or later, turn their eyes upon his kingdom. Indeed, for much of the 880s the *Chronicle* turns an almost obsessive eye upon the activities of a Viking army upon the Continent, as it harried the splintering kingdoms of the grandsons of Charlemagne, inserting itself like a wedge into the political divisions and rivalries that beset

Europe. These were the ideal conditions for a Viking army to exploit, with various factions willing to pay under the table for its services, and those who might have defeated them too distracted by royal rivalries to turn their attention fully upon it. With John the Old Saxon and Grimbald the Frank at his court, Alfred had first-hand accounts of what was happening across the Channel available to him. Thus, with the renewed energy that suffused him after the victory at Edington, Alfred set about reforming the defence of his realm.

Having survived the Viking onslaught, Alfred found himself in a uniquely favourable position for the next few years and he moved, cautiously but firmly, to take full advantage of the situation. Such was the transformative effect of his victory at Edington that the old enmities that had divided the Anglo-Saxon kingdoms from each other seem to have largely dissolved. Wessex and Mercia had been rivals always and enemies often in the centuries before Alfred's reign, but when Ceolwulf, the puppet king of Mercia, was deposed sometime soon after the Battle of Edington, the Mercian witan made no move to raise another king. Instead, in the obscure period when the Chronicler turns his attention obsessively to Viking activities on the Continent and, frustratingly, all but ignores what was happening in Britain, it appears that the magnates of the western half of Mercia, which was not under Viking rule, decided to throw in their lot with Alfred and accept him as overlord. This decision was probably helped by the positions Alfred gave many Mercian clerics at his court; as bishop of Worcester, Werferth was a man of considerable standing in the secular as well as the religious world. By 883, Mercia had accepted Alfred as its overking, for a charter has survived from that year in which Æthelred, the ealdorman of Mercia, makes a grant to Berkeley Abbey to which Alfred gave his assent.

For the rest of Alfred's reign, and on in to the reign of Alfred's son, Æthelred ruled Mercia but as a governor rather than king: in the documents of the time, Æthelred was accorded the title *Myrcna hlaford*, 'Lord of the Mercians', rather than 'rex'. We do not know how Æthelred came to Alfred's attention, but the king of Wessex trusted his Mercian lieutenant completely, so much so that, in the latter half of the 880s, he married his eldest daughter and firstborn child, Æthelflæd, to him.

Mercia had been firmly but tactfully brought under the control of Alfred's house. But it was not the only old enemy that Alfred's growing status and power attracted to him. The princedoms of Wales were remnants of the old kingdoms of the Britons: for centuries they and their ancestors had resisted the westward expansion of the Anglo-Saxon kingdoms – indeed, they resisted much longer and more successfully than their conquerors when faced with the very similar Viking incursions – but in the end the Britons had been pushed into the mountainous western reaches of the island: Cornwall, Wales, Cumbria, Strathclyde. Within Wales, seven princedoms fought vicious little battles, one against the other, when not harrying or being harried by Mercian forces. In this shifting tapestry of alliances, it became clear to all the players that there was a new power that had to be accommodated: Alfred. Through the 880s, one after the other, the princedoms of Wales accepted Alfred as overking, with the weaker kingdoms first seeking his protection against the ambitions of Anarawd ap Rhodri, ruler of the kingdom of Gwynedd. The next pair of kingdoms to seek Alfred's protection sought his help against the advances of the Mercians under Alfred's son-in-law, Æthelred. It was a shrewd move. Sharing the same overking, Æthelred was no longer free to advance his border westwards. The only holdout was Gwynedd, which turned instead, initially, to the only remaining counterforce to Alfred: the Vikings. The alliance with the Northumbrian Vikings provided, as Asser remarked, 'no good, just injury' and finally, by 893, Gwynedd submitted to Alfred too.

The ritual of submission was prescribed by tradition. The supplicant king – a man not wont to make obeisance before anyone – had to bow before Alfred, whereupon the king of the West Saxons placed his hands upon his head, in a manner similar to the consecration of bishops. As important a part of the ritual was the gift giving that then followed, with Alfred showering treasure upon his new underking. The obligations that attended gift giving served to cement the relationship and, since the gifts spread beyond the immediate royal circle, it also served to demonstrate to other Welsh magnates that submitting to a king as rich and munificent as Alfred could be a very profitable exercise for them as well. As an underking, each of these Welsh monarchs vowed to subject 'himself with all his people to King Alfred's lordship on the same conditions as Æthelred and the Mercians, namely that in every respect he would be obedient to the royal will'.[1] But Alfred had a light touch, requiring little from his underkings beyond their formal obeisance and their withholding help from his enemies. Æthelred, lord of the Mercians, had a greater role to play, attending Alfred's court when it was in or near Mercia and playing a crucial role in the next stage of Alfred's consolidation of his realm: the retaking of London.

The sources are frustratingly terse about what Alfred evidently regarded as a major event in his reign. The *Chronicle* merely states that he occupied the city. Asser is more forthcoming, but not really any more useful, saying that Alfred 'restored the city of London splendidly – after so many towns had been burned and so many people slaughtered – and made it habitable again'.[2] Was the retaking of the city a culmination of a campaign not mentioned in the sources or is he referring to past tribulations? We do not know. But we do know, from archaeology, that Alfred transformed the city.

For a long time, historians and archaeologists had puzzled over a statement in Bede about the kingdom of the East Saxons: 'Its capital is the city of London, which stands on the banks of the Thames, and is a trading centre for many nations who visit it by land and sea.'[3].The problem was, there was not the slightest sign of this 'trading centre' in the City of London, the site of Roman London and presumably the site of the capital of the East Saxons. It turned out that it was the presumption that was wrong. The Saxons, ever nervous of the ghost-haunted ruins of the Romans, chose to build their trading centre a little upriver from the old city, in a long, littoral development roughly where the Strand now lies. Alfred, when he took the city, and in keeping with the other major planned developments he was beginning throughout his kingdom, moved London back within the old Roman walls. The king intended London to serve as a fort and base, and the old walls, and the bridge, even in disrepair, provided major obstacles to any Viking fleet attempting to sail up the Thames and into the heart of his expanded kingdom. The memory of the old Saxon settlement was retained however in 'Aldwych'

– literally 'old town' and where archaeologists have found remains of the pre-Alfredian port.

London had always been a Mercian town. When Alfred took it, '[a]ll the English free of Danish rule gave Alfred their loyalty'.[4] The king of the West Saxons was no longer a tribal ruler but the king of the Angles and the Saxons. A nation was moving towards its birth.

Having taken London, and received the formal subjection of everyone 'free of Danish rule', Alfred promptly gave the city into the charge of Æthelred, lord of the Mercians. Although Alfred might be moving towards an ideal of rule that united the once warring tribes of England, he was mindful of the sensibilities of people who might see him as conqueror rather than ruler.

Such tact was necessary as well as sensible. Alfred had, of necessity, to rule much more through persuasion than through force and law. The king was always on the move through his realm, but he could not be everywhere, and rule in his absence devolved upon his officers. In the years before Alfred's reign, there had been a slow but fundamental change in the relationship between a king and his magnates and lesser officers. Land was the fundamental currency of wealth and power in Anglo-Saxon England. Although kings gave gifts of gold, and warriors wore, indeed flaunted, their wealth in arm rings and buckles, yet land was the source of all. In the early centuries of the Anglo-Saxon era, land was a gift too, given in the purview of the king as reward for faithful service to his followers. But, and this was key, the land was a royal gift to a particular individual – it did not pass automatically to his kin on his death. Thus land was loanland, and it returned to the king when its holder died, or failed to serve the king faithfully. Thus a king could reward, and attract, followers. However, while this worked well for a king's secular fellowship, it did not suit the Church. A monastery was not moveable in the same way a warrior's household was. Monks prayed, calling blessings down upon the land they worked and the king they served, and to do this they needed the land to be theirs, to belong to the institution so the institution could endure through the generations. Thus, the idea of bookland developed, land that was held by royal charter. Once entered in the 'book' the land belonged perpetually to the Church. For the king, it was a free gift, given to God in the hope and expectation of receiving God's grace on him and his kingdom.

Not surprisingly, the magnates and officials of Anglo-Saxon England began to ask for their land to be bookland too and thus inheritable, and by the end of ninth century the gift of bookland was seen as the normal reward for faithful service to the king. But, by giving away land in perpetuity, a king also gave away the means by which he had attracted warriors to his cause. How were the kings of Anglo-Saxon England going to maintain their armies with a steadily diminishing land base from which to make grants to retainers?

The solution was gradually worked out by the Mercian kings of the eighth century, in particular Offa (d. 796), the most powerful king of his time. With the gift of bookland came the obligation of the 'common burdens', a threefold military obligation of building and maintaining bridges, defending fortifications against the king's enemies and military service with the king on campaign. Thus land became heritable, but so was the obligation to serve the king – there had been no previous necessity for a man's sons to serve the same lord and many indeed struck out for new courts in the hope of faster advancement. Now, with lands to protect, a magnate, a thegn or a reeve, and his descendants, had a vested interest in the protection and service of the realm of which their land was a part.

When Alfred inherited the kingdom of the West Saxons, he took over a realm in which a particularly high number of magnates and royal officials owned land in their own right, in part because of his father's 'Decimation' of his land, when Æthelwulf had given away one-tenth of his territory before his departure on pilgrimage to Rome. The problems inherent with bookland had exacerbated Alfred's difficulties in dealing with the Great Army, for a magnate who held lands in his own right would be the more tempted to cut a deal with a force he judged to be the coming power in the kingdom, and thus save his lands from appropriation. Having won victory at Edington, Alfred had the luxury of some time in which to reorganise defence of his realm: he used it to extraordinary effect, and in the process set the country upon the path that led to a unitary state.

The key strategic advantage of the Great Heathen Army was mobility and surprise. When faced with the assembled forces of an Anglo-Saxon kingdom, a Viking force was far more likely to take refuge behind fortifications or even take to its boats than risk everything in a full-scale battle. But the time taken to assemble the fyrd, and the limited time in which it could remain on campaign, meant that any half-competent Viking commander could raid and depart before anything much could be done about it. Even the Great Army, set upon conquest rather than raiding, used the same tactics, picking its time and place to strike, and often waiting for times in the calendar when its enemies were occupied with harvest or festivals.

As always, Alfred dug deep into the problem he faced, working down to first principles. He saw that, to counter the mobility of a Viking army, he required forces that could be assembled quickly and move fast: he needed a mounted standing army. This was a radical change from Anglo-Saxon practice, and one that would be far more costly to the magnates required to provide the mounted troops, but by 893, when the *Chronicle* describes in passing the results of the changes the king had inaugurated, Alfred had persuaded, cajoled, suborned and wheedled his nobility into line:

> The king's army reforms kept half the warriors on duty and half in reserve, apart from the garrisons.[5]

Rather than a lengthy assembly, Alfred and his magnates always had half the realm's warriors ready for immediate action. We know this force was mounted because, in its description of the actions and campaigns of the 890s, the *Chronicle* repeatedly refers to Alfred's forces riding after the Viking army. The horses were not the great war beasts of the high medieval period but smaller animals, not that much larger than ponies, but ideal for transporting the relatively lightly armed warrior of the time.

By retaining half the warriors in reserve, that is, still living in their landholdings, Alfred also ensured the maintenance of the king's peace, for these warriors fulfilled the function of a police force as well as an army, deterring bands of brigands from raiding the small farming communities and religious establishments that dotted the land. Having men in place on the ground also meant that those on service were less likely to go running back to their homes to look after hearth and family.

But this mobile strike force was only half the solution. Even with a mounted army, the Viking mastery of amphibious operations meant they could still achieve first strike along the long coastline of Wessex, or along its navigable rivers. To protect against the sudden threat of the dragon ships appearing on the horizon, Alfred had to improve the defences of his kingdom and make them accessible to his people. To that end, he set about the most sustained programme of building since the Romans had conquered Britain seven centuries earlier.

Alfred built fortresses, or burhs (from which comes 'borough'), right across his kingdom, each of them carefully placed in a strategic location. But these were not simply defences, rather fortified towns, able to function economically and independently, yet able to combine with each other to form a defensive screen across Wessex. The thirty burhs were placed so that no one and no place in Wessex was more than twenty miles – or a day's march – away from a refuge. The burhs defended harbours, rivers, Roman roads and the old trackways of Britain. Where Roman or Iron Age forts already existed, Alfred was perfectly happy to reuse and renovate what was on the ground, but where there was nothing he built from scratch. Although we don't know for certain, it seems likely that Alfred made use of his new standing army in the construction of the burhs since, as any commander knows, one of the most difficult of tasks is keeping bored men occupied and out of mischief – digging ditches and raising palisades would have served that end admirably. Most of the new burhs were built near Alfred's existing royal vills. These were already strongholds, but with what was essentially a fortified town near a royal estate, each helped to defend and support the other.

Bitter experience had taught Alfred that there were two main avenues of attack for Viking armies: the long, exposed south coast of Wessex, running from Cornwall to Kent, and the kingdom's northern border, the River Thames. The river we see today is a narrow, constricted waterway in comparison to the broad, tidal expanse it used to be. The first London Bridge, built by the Romans, crossed the river from a small gravel hill near its current site in the City of London to a natural causeway through the swamp marshes of Southwark. The river ebbed and flowed with the tide, swelling to half a mile wide at high tide. Even at low tide it was wider than the fast flowing, narrow stream we see today. Such a wide expanse of water, even though it was shallow, was an ideal route into the heart of Wessex for Viking longboats. So Alfred set about stopping them. He built burhs in Southwark, Sashes, Wallingford and Cricklade along the river. On the coast, the burhs at Bridport, Portchester, Exeter and elsewhere were sited to guard the mouths of rivers or the most secure harbours. Inland burhs such as the ones at Winchester and Wilton dominated the Roman road system and guarded the ancient trackways of Britain. Thus Alfred had created a system of defence in depth, with his mobile army able to use the burhs as bases for resupply and to launch attacks on Viking forces, while the burh garrisons were on hand to harass smaller Viking foraging parties.

One of the key strengths of the burh system was its ability to prevent a Viking army getting away with its plunder. Such was the advantage the Vikings had in mobility that it was always possible a raiding party could land somewhere and ravage into the interior of the kingdom. But nothing slowed and dispersed an army so much as having to transport its plunder back to its ships, and that gave the burhs the chance to launch raids upon its scattered units, while the sequestering of resources in the burhs made it much more difficult for Viking foragers to keep their army supplied.

A swift striking force might have been tempted to simply leave the burhs untouched, but doing so meant lines of communication became vulnerable to attack. However, Viking raiding armies had neither the equipment nor the know-how to take a burh, so their only expedient was to attempt to starve the garrison into submission. But doing so sacrificed the Vikings' chief operational advantage, mobility, and allowed the neighbouring garrisons and the field force to gather and break the siege – and the besieging army.

But perhaps nowhere is Alfred's practical genius more clearly demonstrated than in the thought he put into making these burhs viable defensive units. It was all very well building forts, but unless they were continually manned and defended they would prove a serious liability. The military protocol for a marauding Viking army was first to secure a defensive position with good lines of communication and access to water for a fast exit; Alfred was building a series of these right across his country. If he failed to organise forces to defend them properly, he was in effect building the means for the Vikings to succeed on their next attempt to conquer Wessex.

A burh was not just a fortress, but a planned town – the people living in the town provided much of the manpower to defend the burh, and ensured that it would be defended and guarded. In some cases, such as at Winchester, Alfred was simply expanding what was already there but in others he created a town on a greenfield site. For the burh to remain effective as a defensive bastion it had to be a viable economic unit, and land was allocated to each for its supply and provision. But, possibly as a side effect – although, with Alfred, it's hard not to suspect he may have thought of this too – the building of protected settlements with concentrations of population had the result of kick-starting towns, and their attendant trade and wealth creation, into existence. Although there's very little left of Alfred's original burhs, the street plan of somewhere like Wallingford, with its regular grid, probably dates from its foundation. If so, it shows just how ambitious Alfred's building programme was, for Wallingford covered 100 acres (forty hectares): the king had created, from scratch, the second-biggest town in his kingdom.

In order to support each burh, Alfred and his children, who continued and expanded the burhs as they slowly reconquered the land the Great Heathen Army had taken, created a system of administration that ensured sufficient land and resources were allocated to each burh, both for its maintenance and its defence. Our main evidence for this is a document called the *Burghal Hidage*, which probably dates from the reign of Alfred's son, but which indicates the administrative planning that went into the creation of each burh. The *Burghal Hidage* lists the forts created through Wessex, and states how much taxable land (assessed in terms of 'hides') was assigned to each:

> For the maintenance and defence of an acre's breadth of wall, sixteen hides are required. If every hide is represented by one, then every pole [5.5 yards] of wall can be manned by four men. Then, for the maintenance of twenty poles of wall, eighty hides are required by the same reckoning I have stated above … For the maintenance of a circuit of twelve furlongs of wall, 1920 hides are required. If the circuit is greater, the additional amount can easily be deduced from this amount, for 160 men are always required for one furlong, then every pole of wall is manned by four men.[6]

So one hide of land was expected to produce enough to support one member of the burh garrison. An average-sized burh required, by this formula, 900 men to garrison it. The land around the burh and, in particular, the landholders had to equip and provide the men for the burh.

This was a huge undertaking, and one that only the near disaster of 878 allowed Alfred to impose upon his magnates and landholders. Even so, there was a certain amount of reluctance and Alfred must have spent a large part of the decade after the Battle of Edington travelling his kingdom, cajoling and persuading his magnates to undertake the extraordinary building programme their king had imposed upon them. There was little Alfred could do to force his magnates to do his will – he had to persuade them.

That they were reluctant is hardly surprising. The money Alfred had raised to pay off the Great Heathen Army in 871 had been a great drain on the finances of his magnates, both secular and clerical, and further sums had been paid over in the defence against Guthrum's assault from 876 to 878. Now Alfred was asking them to help provide for the building or repair of thirty burhs, to provide and supply a total garrison for the burhs of nearly 30,000 men and all this while maintaining a mobile field army year round. It was a huge increase in the royal demands upon its moneyed and landed classes, and only the constant threat of Viking attack made it acceptable. But, grumbling and reluctant though they were, the magnates of Wessex largely did as they were asked. They built and maintained the new fortresses. They provided men for Alfred's army. And they waited for the Vikings to return.

10

Back to the Barricades

The Chronicler may have looked back on the decade of the 880s as a time of peace but it probably did not look that way to villagers who lived near the coast or estuaries. The original Great Army may have settled down to raise children, but the army that had made a temporary base in Fulham in 878 – causing Guthrum to abandon Chippenham in haste to look to his own holdings in East Anglia – was busy on the Continent, where it drew the horrified but fascinated gaze of the Chronicler. With the unerring Viking nose for political instability, war bands had gathered in Francia to profit and plunder from the chaos that followed the successive deaths of Charles the Bald (877), his son, Louis the Stammerer (879), and Charles's grandson Louis III and his nephew, Louis the Younger (both 882). It was the perfect landscape for raiders and war bands to exploit, and the chronicles of the Franks lamented the devastation caused:

Never do the Northmen cease to take captive and kill Christian people, to destroy churches and ramparts, to burn out houses in flames. Through all the open streets the dead are lying – priests, laymen, nobles, women, youth and little children.[1]

The situation faced by the Franks was of a different order to the raiding that continued throughout the 880s on the other side of the Channel. Of course, if you were unlucky enough to be caught up in a raid and have your livestock stolen or your children captured for the slave markets, your view of the peace was likely to have been more jaundiced. It was probably such complainants that led the translator of Orosius's *Histories Against the Pagans*, a member of Alfred's scholarly circle, to say how it was 'exceedingly disgraceful to us that we complain about what we now call war, when strangers and foreigners come upon us, despoil us a little and then, soon after, leave again; and we are unwilling to think upon what it was like when no one could even purchase his life from another'.[2] For us today, secure in a comfortable world, it might not seem unreasonable to complain about being despoiled a little, but Alfred and his circle knew well the difference between casual raiding and a full-scale Viking assault. Various passing references, in charters and the *Chronicle*, show us that all was certainly not quiet in this decade of 'peace'. The king retook London definitively in 886, but may have besieged the city also in 883. The king and his forces fought in Surrey in 882, presumably tackling a raiding party. The kingdom's ealdormen were certainly on guard too against Viking incursions, but these actions were the everyday matters of a war-ravaged age, and barely drew the Chronicler's attention. In fact, only two military events during the decade draw more than the most passing of mentions, one for reason of its size and potential danger, the other for its rarity.

First, the unusual action. In 882

> Alfred took a fleet out to sea, attacked four Danish ships and took two of them, killing the crews. The other two ships surrendered after heavy losses in killed and wounded.[3]

The *Chronicle* only mentions four naval actions for the whole ninth century; Alfred took part in three of them. His analytical mind had early come to the conclusion that the best way to secure his kingdom was to stop Viking armies reaching it in the first place, but although his analysis was correct – and would prove the basis for later British power – it was beyond the naval technology of the time to intercept ships at sea and destroy them. When naval battles did occur, and they were rare, they were essentially land battles on floating wooden platforms. The vessels themselves did not have the capacity to cause long-range damage to each other, nor were they equipped to ram and sink. Instead, the boats would draw closer to each other, firing what arrows and missiles they had, until, lashed together, the struggle turned into a brutal hand-to-hand affair. Four ships were a raid, not an army, but for the hard-pressed people of Wessex they were four ships that were not going to harry their land after all.

The Vikings launched an altogether more serious assault on Kent in 885.

> The Viking army split in two. One division went east into Europe; the other came and laid siege to Rochester, building

themselves defensive works. The garrison held out until King Alfred brought up the army. The enemy took to their ships, abandoned their camp and horses, and sailed back across the Channel.[4]

Rochester was not one of Alfred's new burhs, but evidently its defences had also been strengthened, so much so that the Viking army was unable to storm it. Settling down to a siege, the Vikings must have assumed that they had the usual long period of time to press their siege while Alfred raised an army. But, with his new standing forces, Alfred was able to launch a surprise attack on the Viking camp, leading the army to run in desperation for its boats. It was a perfect demonstration of the effectiveness of Alfred's new strategy: delay the attackers, then attack in turn.

However, the presence of a fresh army on the shores of Britain was too much for some of the Vikings in East Anglia; despite Guthrum's promises, an army marched south to join the forces at Rochester. Although the sturdy defence by the people of Rochester and Alfred's swift response prevented the two armies joining forces, it persuaded Alfred that he needed to demonstrate to the Vikings of East Anglia that there were consequences to breaking the treaty. And he chose to do so in the Viking manner: he sent a raiding fleet from Kent. The punitive expedition was initially successful, attacking and capturing sixteen Viking craft in the estuary of the River Stour, but, outraged by this attempt to turn their tactics back on them, the Vikings of East Anglia launched every ship they had available and intercepted the Kentish fleet as it sailed back home, defeating it. The *Chronicle* makes no mention of how many ships got back home. Alfred's military mistake meant men died; the *Chronicle*, while not ignoring Alfred's mistakes, certainly gave them less play than his victories.

Despite the Vikings of East Anglia succumbing to the temptation to go raiding, so long as Guthrum remained king there was a check on them. And as the reigning power, with a foot in Anglo-Saxon society, Guthrum certainly had no wish to host a fresh Viking army on his territory; men eager for loot and conquest made uncertain guests. But in 890, the man who had come so close to being Alfred's nemesis and the doom of Anglo-Saxon England died.

The *Chronicle* records Guthrum's death tersely: 'And the northern king, Guthrum, whose baptismal name was Æthelstan, died. He was King Alfred's godson, and he lived in East Anglia and was the first [of the Danes] to settle that land.'

Despite occasional difficulties, Alfred could take some considerable satisfaction in the way he had integrated Guthrum into the religious, political and cultural framework of the country. But with the paramount king of the Vikings dead, the way was now clear for a new Viking warlord to make a bid for the final kingdom in the land and to earn himself a crown. In Wessex, Alfred prepared for the storm he saw gathering on the horizon. He had enjoyed twelve years of relative peace. It would not last much longer.

The forces that were ravaging Francia in the 880s were greater than any Alfred had faced before. In 886, the war bands converged on Paris in such numbers that the city's defenders, watching, appalled, from atop their towers, saw longboats covering the River Seine to the horizon. The Vikings besieged the city for more than a year, only leaving when Charles the Fat bought them off with 700 lb (318 kg) of silver and permission to ravage Burgundy.

With such riches available in Francia, there was little incentive for the war bands to move on. But what the divided rulers of the Franks could not achieve, nature could. A blight devastated the region in 892, and famine stalked the bare fields. Even Viking ravagers could not ravage what was not there, but they still managed to get their victims to pay for their leaving: the Franks provided 250 boats to ship their persecutors anywhere but there. So, in the autumn of 892, the Viking fleet set sail. They did not have far to go.

There is no more familiar shape to us today than the coastline of Britain. But that coastline is a human creation, with most of the reclamation work taking place between the seventeenth and nineteenth centuries. Before then, the coast of England in particular was very different. Some place names tell of the change: the Isle of Ely, the Isle of Thanet, the Isle of Oxney, indeed, the Isle of Athelney. These were islands amid salt marsh and shifting sand, small tussocks of raised ground that stood above the tide flood. Whole counties were once all but islands, such as the lost kingdom of Lindsey – roughly equivalent to Lincolnshire – and the Wash was not a bite out of England's bump but an abscess of marsh and swamp that covered most of Cambridgeshire and Lincolnshire. On the Kent and Sussex border, the River Rother flowed into the vast expanse of the Romney Marsh, its broad, flat flow tidal and navigable up to where Bodiam Castle stands today, a relic of defence against a later cross-Channel invasion. There was no castle standing there when the Viking fleet sailed up the river, but the Northmen took a half-completed burh before making a permanent camp on the other side of the marsh, at Appledore. With access to the sea, and protection on land from surprise attack provided by the great forest of Andredsweald, which then stretched from Kent right through the North Downs, the vanguard had made a secure base from which to prosecute the campaign to conquer Wessex. That they were bent on conquest is apparent from the fact that the fleet carried not only warriors but their families – these were men who intended to stay.

While this vanguard was the greater in terms of numbers, it was probably not the command fleet. For while it established itself on the south coast, in a classic Viking pincer movement, a second fleet of eighty ships rounded Kent and landed on its north coast at Milton Regis, near Sittingbourne, just south of the Isle of Sheppey. Again, the site had been carefully chosen, allowing for a swift retreat if necessity demanded, but with good lines of sight against attack and easily dug defences. There were now Viking armies encamped in strongly defended positions on the north and south coasts of Kent, able to strike out inland and by sea.

The Chronicler does not name the commander of the army camped at Appledore, but the leader of the smaller fleet he does name, and it was a name to conjure fear in whoever heard it: Hæsten. Between 859 and 862, Hæsten had commanded the legendary Viking raid that rounded Spain, sailed through the straits of Gibraltar and harried northern Africa and southern France, and on to Italy, with its ultimate aim being to sack Rome. Although, in the end, they did not get as far as Rome, the range, daring and bravado showed by Hæsten then had put him into the first rank of Viking commanders. In the years afterward Hæsten had led forces in Brittany and northern Francia, reaping further riches, and demonstrating a propensity, remarkable even in a Viking, for breaking solemn oaths. But a crown had escaped him. Now, with an army greater than any that had attacked Britain before, it was Hæsten's chance to claim one.

For Alfred, this was the test. He had reorganised his defences, physical and spiritual. He had created an army and built burhs. He had set to work rebuilding his people's relationship with God in order to regain heaven's favour. Now he would see if his analysis was right.

The king responded quickly. Sending messengers to the Viking rulers of East Anglia and Northumbria, demanding their neutrality in the coming conflict, Alfred marched his field force into Kent and took up position in between Appledore in the south and Milton Regis in the north. Thus positioned, Alfred could pursue either army should it attempt a breakout, while his patrols harassed Viking foraging parties and cut the overland communication between the two Viking armies.

Of the two armies, the one led by Hæsten, although smaller, had taken the more dangerous position. Milton Regis lay on Watling Street, the Roman road. At a stroke, Hæsten had cut communication between Rochester and Canterbury. The road provided a clear line of march either west to London or east to the foremost ecclesiastical centre in England. Furthermore, a prehistoric track ran from just south of the Viking camp across the North Downs to Winchester in the heart of Wessex (it's now called the Pilgrims' Way as it later became a favourite route for votaries travelling to the shrine of St Thomas Becket in Canterbury). Add to this Hæsten's renown as a Viking commander and it is little surprise that Alfred identified his force as the greater threat. With Hæsten content to remain behind his fortifications, Alfred turned to diplomacy. After all, in the end, that had worked with Guthrum.

At some point during the year, Alfred, with his son-in-law Ealdorman Æthelred, the lord of the Mercians, met Hæsten for face-to-face negotiations. Alfred had previous, and bitter, experience of treaty talks with Vikings, but nevertheless he must have judged Hæsten's protestations of peaceful intent sufficiently convincing for him to join in a peace pledge, and one sanctified, in Alfred's eyes at least, by the king and his son-in-law, Æthelred, standing as godfathers to Hæsten's two young sons as they were baptised. For his part, Hæsten handed over hostages and gave oaths of good conduct, presumably keeping his fingers firmly crossed behind his back as he received the rich gifts from Alfred that were his due following the pledge giving and baptism. Treasure obtained, Hæsten promptly sailed across the Thames Estuary and made a new, even more secure base at Benfleet in Essex, from which he set out raiding the territory of the Mercians – the land of his son's godfather. History does not record the fate a weary Alfred accorded the hostages Hæsten had left in his hands. Their lives, of course, were forfeit, but Alfred's later behaviour, when people whom Hæsten really would not have wanted to lose fell into his hands, suggests that he might have been more merciful than the hostages could have expected.

Viking campaigns, unlike the brief but savage wars between the Anglo-Saxon kingdoms, were long-winded affairs. The Vikings had learned that one of their best strategies was to simply wait things out from behind their fortifications. Sooner or later, the king's fyrd would drift away, returning to their land and their farms, and the king would be forced to buy them off while he still had an army left. To that end, the Viking army in Appledore sat tight, sending out foraging parties that both replenished supplies and probed the battle readiness of Alfred's forces. With Alfred camped in between the two forces, there can have been little communication between them, save by boat. However, Hæsten no doubt let the southern Vikings know about his relocation to Benfleet. Further communication also passed between the Appledore Vikings and the Viking kingdoms of East Anglia and Northumbria. Despite their pledges, and the six hostages the East Anglians had given to Alfred in surety of their neutrality, the lure of loot and conquest was too much for these newly settled freebooters. Even if their kings had wanted to maintain the peace, the Viking kingdoms had little way of stopping independent action; any man with a boat and a following could take the whale road and join the feeding frenzy that was about to fall upon the last un-plundered kingdom of England. So, as the Appledore Vikings broke camp around Easter 873, some one hundred ships from Northumbria and East Anglia sailed south down the North Sea and then west along the Channel. Alfred was about to be faced with the great dread of every general: a multi-front war.

A multi-front war is also the great dread of every historian: making sense of a series of messy events inevitably entails imposing a greater sense of order and succession on what occurred than would ever have been perceptible to the men fighting the campaigns, when confusion must have reigned for much of the next few months, but history aims to clarify, not confuse. So, bearing in mind this warning, let's try to work a path through what happened next.

The Chronicler seems either to have always regarded the Appledore Vikings as a lesser threat, or their leader was simply never well known, for he is never named in the sources. But whoever he was, by Easter 873 he and his army had spent a year in England to little profit; his men must have been getting restless, and word had reached him of Hæsten's dealings with Alfred and his move to Benfleet in Essex. It was time for some Viking action.

Sending their boats round Kent and up the Thames Estuary to Mersea, a tidal island in Essex that was in friendly hands, the Appledore Vikings broke camp en masse and marched out on a full-scale pillaging raid. Edward the Elder, Alfred's son, was in charge of the nearest Wessex fyrd which was camped somewhere around Maidstone, but the Appledore Vikings evaded or killed the pickets they first encountered, using the great Andredsweald forest as cover for their breakout into the rich farmlands of Hampshire, Surrey and Berkshire. There, the pent-up frustration of a year confined in the marshes of Romney was unleashed in a fury of pillaging, with raiding parties scouring the farms and villages of the shires around the main Viking army. But, in the end, their own greed overwhelmed them. So laden with loot was the army that its progress north slowed to a crawl, allowing Edward the Elder to catch up. The Appledore Vikings were already meeting stiffer resistance from the local militias manning the burhs of Hampshire and Surrey, and having to set up temporary fortifications as they went. Slowed down by a wagon train of loot and the attacks of burh militias, Edward finally caught the Appledore Vikings at Farnham in Surrey. The unnamed Viking king was badly injured in the ensuing battle and, with their chief down, the survivors fled in rout, abandoning their ravages in an attempt to reach safety. But even without the loot, the badly mauled Viking army could not get to safety. Instead, they were forced to make a miserable last-ditch refuge on an island in the River Thames near Iver in Buckinghamshire. Wounded, exhausted and with their plunder gone, the forlorn remnant of the Viking army watched as the forces of Wessex took up positions around them. Starvation waited upon them.

But on this occasion, fortune favoured the Vikings. Edward's army had exhausted its own provisions and his men had come to the end of their time of service with the field army. It was time for them to return to their homes and fields and defend them. Edward, unable to feed his men, had no choice but to let them go. Alfred was on his way, marching with a relief army, but they would not arrive in time, and Edward was left with only the men of his personal retinue to hold the siege in place. If Ealdorman Æthelred had not arrived with reinforcements from London, it could have gone badly for the young ætheling. But with them in place, Edward was able to negotiate from a position of strength. He no longer had the men to storm the Viking-held island, but they had missed the chance to break out. It was in both parties' interest to agree a way out, and that they did, with the Vikings allowed to withdraw and limp east into Essex, shadowed into Viking territory by Edward and his men. For the Appledore Vikings, the raid had been an almost complete disaster: their king badly wounded (he is not mentioned again, so he may have later succumbed to his wounds), many men killed and injured, and precisely nothing to set against the losses except their lives. For Edward, and Alfred, the raid had shown the strength but also the weakness of their defences. The defence in depth provided by the burhs had harassed the Vikings all along the way and slowed them down enough for Edward and the field army to catch them. But they still did not have the logistics in place to support an army travelling fast and away from its support, nor could they call up reinforcements quickly enough to ram home the advantage the victory at Farnham had provided.

But there was no time to do anything about the deficiencies. As Alfred, with the fresh shift of the Wessex fyrd, marched towards London, word reached him that the opportunist fleet that had set sail from Northumbria and East Anglia had landed. With Alfred and Edward caught up with trying to deal with the incursion in Hampshire, Surrey and Berkshire, these seaborne raiders had sailed west along the Channel and landed one army near Exeter and another, having rounded Cornwall, on the north coast of Devon, hard by one of Alfred's burhs. If they could take and make secure coastal fortifications on the north and south coasts of Devon, the Vikings would have the perfect base from which to ravage the west of Wessex, and the opportunity too, what with Alfred and Edward occupied in the east.

It was a critical moment. Hæsten realised it too, and started to send parties of reavers into Mercia from his base in Benfleet, thus attempting to draw away the support Alfred could have expected from the lord of the Mercians.

Assailed in the west, raided in the east, at least Alfred knew that his son had dealt with and dispatched the Appledore army. Judging the threat in the west the greatest, Alfred took most of his forces on a fast march into Devon to relieve the siege of Exeter. He sent a small part of his army on to London, to tell the officials there of his actions and to advise them that they needed to take their defence into their own hands for the moment.

The men of London, possibly bolstered by Ealdorman Æthelred and Mercian forces, did more than that. Rather than waiting for the Vikings to come to them, they marched out from London, heading to Hæsten's base in Benfleet. The veteran Viking commander had become complacent; joining the raiding parties himself, he had left too light a guard on his base camp. The Londoners took the defenders by surprise, killing those they found in the open and storming the fortifications after a short, fierce fight. Hæsten had left his plunder, his boats, and his women and children in Benfleet. The Londoners plundered in turn, reclaiming much of what Hæsten had taken and taking captive, for sale as slaves or to be redeemed for ransom, the women and children they found in the camp. Foremost among the captives were Hæsten's own wife and sons, the very same sons Alfred and Ealdorman Æthelred had stood sponsor to as godfathers when the boys were baptised. Almost as significant were the boats. The triumphant Londoners sailed the best of them back to London. The rest, they burnt.

It must have seemed like a decisive victory at the time, but Hæsten and the bulk of his men were still at large, and now they had added incentive to reave, for they had lost the yield of the previous year's plunder and were, effectively, starting from scratch. Furthermore, there was revenge. They had lost women, children, comrades. For Hæsten, there was the realisation that his wife and sons would be taken to Alfred, to dispose of as he saw fit. He must have expected as little mercy as he would have shown had the circumstances been reversed. But in this, as in so much else, Alfred astonishes. When Hæsten's wife and sons were eventually brought to him, he returned them to the Viking leader, unharmed and without ransom or pledge. As his godson, however little attention Hæsten paid to that, Alfred saw the boy as his own spiritual son and thus no more to be used as a pawn than his own children.

But this lay in the future. When Hæsten and his raiding parties returned to the wreckage at Benfleet, the Viking chief, reinforced by a contingent from the defeated Appledore Vikings who wanted to try their luck again and further boatloads of excited men from East Anglia and Northumbria, decided to build a new base at Shoeburyness, east of Benfleet. He might have lost wife and sons, but he had not lost his desire for treasure. Nor had he lost his boldness. Hæsten was the man who had led a fleet into the Mediterranean, pillaging Christian and Muslim alike. With the east of the country picked clean and wary, he determined to make the boldest strike possible. Using the boats his reinforcements had brought with them, Hæsten made a cross-country dash, sailing up the Thames – it's not clear how he got past the burhs on the river but he evidently did – and then, via tributaries and portage, on to the great western waterway of the country, the River Severn. It was an extraordinary feat of strength, speed and endurance; the Viking army had travelled 185 miles as the crow flies, and much further by water, through hostile territory before finally building a fortified camp at Buttington (near Welshpool), on the border of Mercia and the kingdom of Gwynedd. As in Francia, Hæsten was trying to insinuate himself into the political and military cracks between kingdoms.

It did not work. Although Alfred was occupied with the Viking forces in Devon, his ealdormen shadowed and followed Hæsten's army as it went, tracking it all the way and then, when they knew where it had settled, they assembled the men of Mercia, those from the Wessex shires not keeping pressure on the Devon Vikings, and the forces of Powys, Alfred's British allies. Rather than dividing the kingdoms of Britain, Hæsten was uniting them against him.

The army that confronted Hæsten was far larger than anything he had expected. The Vikings had made camp on an island in the river. The combined English and Welsh forces laid siege for weeks, forcing the desperate Vikings, who had had no chance to forage supplies, to eat their own horses. Faced with the realisation that starvation would soon rob his men of the strength to fight, Hæsten led a desperate breakout attempt.

Both sides suffered great losses, but Hæsten escaped, and enough men made it with him for the Viking chief to make a fighting retreat back to his base at Shoeburyness. While he had been defeated again, Hæsten was still not beaten. Although winter was drawing close, Hæsten tried once more. Fresh recruits from Northumbria and East Anglia, apparently undeterred by the lack of success until now, had streamed into his base and so, abandoning boats for horse and feet, Hæsten led a forced march west again, across Mercia, to the old Roman city of Chester. The Roman roads allowed the Vikings to make quick time to the ruined city, where they again set about strengthening their defences, but the response was as swift as before. Although the Vikings had moved too fast to be caught and brought to battle in the open, the mounted infantry of Mercia and Wessex arrived at Chester soon after Hæsten and, with grim determination, immediately set about a scorched earth policy, burning or feeding to their own horses all the foodstuff in the region. Having been starved out once, Hæsten was not about to suffer the same fate again, and he led his forces out of Mercia, into the territory of Gwynedd, until recently allied to the Viking kingdom based in York. The previous alliance brought the princes of Gwynedd no joy, for Hæsten needed plunder to pay off his men, and he was not fussy where he found it. Through the winter of 894, Hæsten's forces tried to make up for their mauling by taking what they could from Gwynedd and then, as the weather improved, they made their way back to base in Essex. But rather than risk further entanglement with the armies of Mercia and Wessex, Hæsten and his men took the long, safe route back, staying at all times in Viking-held territory. Hæsten, the daring captain of the raid into the Mediterranean and the scourge of Francia, had had enough of Wessex.

For his part, Alfred had spent a year in the field, slowly wearing down the Viking forces in Devon. This was a war of attrition, of patrols against foraging parties, of vigilance and watchfulness, and in the end Alfred's patience paid off. The Vikings who had sailed from Northumbria and East Anglia a year before in hope of plunder and excitement had gathered precious little and they resolved to return to their halls. But even their sailing home met with disaster, as an opportunist attack on the Sussex coast was met by the garrison of the burh at Chichester and routed, with hundreds of men never to make it back to their halls.

Having secured his western shires, Alfred returned east. Then, a year and more after they were taken captive, the captured wife and sons of Hæsten were brought before the king. When faced with his godson, Alfred chose not to visit the sins of the father upon the sons. Nor did he return evil on Hæsten's wife. He returned them all to the Viking chief.

We do not know what Hæsten made of this entirely unexpected mercy. He was an immensely experienced warrior, hardened by a life of raiding and slave taking, so seeing the wife and sons he had given up for lost must have been a complete surprise. Although, as we shall see, the forces Hæsten had led continued to campaign against Alfred, it may be significant that Hæsten himself is not mentioned again by the Chronicler. Maybe the old campaigner, reunited with his family, was touched by Alfred's kindness and, taking ship, sailed into a wealthy retirement. He had been raiding for some forty years by this time. One wonders if anything similar had ever happened to him.

Of course, it is possible that Hæsten simply chose to regard the return of his wife and sons as evidence of Alfred's weakness, and decided to keep on fighting, with the Chronicler drawing a veil over his further involvement to spare embarrassment to Alfred's reputation. But, as happened with the Great Heathen Army and Great Summer Army before, it was certainly possible for the leadership of a Viking army to change but for the army to remain in the field. The commander of the Viking forces for the remainder of this campaign has no name in the sources.

Whoever led the Viking forces now had determined on a new strategy. Leaving their Essex stronghold, in the last months of

894, the Vikings sailed a little way up the Thames and then took the River Lea, which joins the Thames east of the City of London, and sailed north, making camp near Hertford. This is wetland, with the rivers Rib, Beane and Mimran joining the Lea here, and the water-crossed land allowed secure fortifications to be built. Set, as they were, north of London, the Vikings were in position to launch fresh raids into Mercia and against London. In the summer of 875, Alfred's officials in London led an attack on the Viking camp in Hertford but it was repulsed with heavy losses. Arriving with his own army at the end of the summer, Alfred realised that the Vikings were poised to seize the harvests that fed London and thus starve the town. Using his men as harvest guards, he ensured the crops were brought in, while he himself searched for a choke point. For although the Vikings, by their location, were a poised threat, if he could cut their river access back to the Thames they would be trapped. Surveying the River Lea, Alfred found what he was looking for a few miles downstream and set his men building a double burh, either side of the river.

Realising they were in danger of being trapped, and with no wish at this point to risk an open battle, the Vikings abandoned their boats and force marched west again, hoping to outdistance Alfred to the point that his supply chains broke and he had to abandon the field. The Viking army made it to Bridgnorth in Shropshire and set about building a winter camp. Yet again, the Viking army had slipped the trap. But, yet again, they had nothing to show for their efforts.

Maybe Hæsten had indeed abandoned the campaign, for the final Viking effort to conquer Alfred's Wessex simply dribbled away. The army in Bridgnorth disbanded in the summer of

896, the discouraged remnants of the forces that had arrived in 892 set on taking a kingdom either settling in Northumbria and East Anglia, or 'those who were still penniless scrounged some ships and went back to their old life across the Channel, raiding up and down the Seine'.[5]

The third and final test faced by Alfred and his kingdom was over. After tracing the troubles faced by the kingdom during this final assault in great detail, the Chronicler reflected on how the king's reformed Wessex had fared:

> The Viking army had not – by God's grace! – afflicted the English people to a very great extent; but they were much more severely afflicted during those three years by the mortality of cattle and men, and most of all by the fact that many of the best king's thegns who were in the land died during those three years.[6]

When reflecting back on an assault that had been greater in numbers than either the Great Heathen Army or the Great Summer Army, and one that, at various points, seemed to be launching attacks from all points of the compass, Alfred, his son Edward and son-in-law Æthelred, lord of the Mercians, as well as all the king's ealdormen and reeves, must have reflected on a job well done. Where before Viking armies had raided deep into the heart of Wessex, striking seemingly at will, on this occasion all but the Appledore Vikings had been restricted to bases on the coast, and the one raid that had penetrated deep into the kingdom had turned into a disaster for the raiders. Hæsten, among the most legendary of Viking leaders, had at various points been reduced to eating his own horses and accepting, as gifts, his own wife and children back from Alfred. In the end, rendered impotent by Alfred's defences, the Vikings had been reduced to pillaging an erstwhile ally and then taking the long route back home through friendly territory to avoid Alfred's land. When raiding, a Viking leader sought, in increasing order of importance, territory, treasure and glory. Hæsten had got none of the first, little of the second and, despite his repeated efforts, only frustration for the third.

Alfred himself had played a relatively smaller role in this final campaign. His part had mainly been to neutralise the threat to the western shires of Wessex, a campaign that had taken over a year to accomplish. The greater role had been played by Edward, Alfred's elder son, who was about twenty at the time, Ealdorman Æthelred, lord of the Mercians, and the various experienced ealdormen in charge of the shires of Wessex. But the strategy they employed, of defence in depth, harrying Viking raiding parties, and maintaining a standing army in the field, was Alfred's. The communication that evidently passed between Alfred and his various commanders may also indicate another benefit of Alfred's reforms: the king could send written orders to his commanders.

Of course, even a successfully prosecuted war tends to produce an aftermath of low-level chaos and, amid the chronic instability of the ninth century, this tendency was exacerbated. The Chronicler tells us that after the disbanding of the main Viking army, the south coast of Wessex was still raided by parties of men from East Anglia and Northumbria; evidently the excitement raised by having another great army present had been too much for many recently settled men, and they had taken to their ships again for a season of looting before returning to their halls. Ever the innovator, Alfred responded by designing his own warships. As naval engagements of the day were essentially infantry battles on floating wooden platforms, Alfred decided to make his ships bigger than the Viking long boats, with sixty oars or more, and higher, so archers could shoot down into the boat alongside, and more stable, making them a better platform. The ideas were sound in principle, but the one occasion where the Chronicler described a naval action involving Alfred's new fleet suggests that there were drawbacks to the new design.

Six boats were raiding the Isle of Wight and the south coast of Devon, so Alfred ordered his new fleet of nine vessels to sea to intercept them. They caught the Vikings in an estuary, blocking the exit to the sea. The three manned boats, guarding the mouth of the estuary, were attacked and two captured. The crews of the other three Viking boats were out raiding, their boats beached, and they returned to find that the ebbing tide had beached the boats of the English too, with three caught on sand near their own vessels and the rest isolated on the far side of the estuary. Realising their desperate situation, the Vikings ran over the sand and mud and engaged in a desperate hand-to-hand struggle with the crew of the three English boats nearby, during which both crews took heavy casualties. But it was a struggle terminated by the inflow of the tide. The Viking boats, being lighter, floated first and their surviving crews rowed them out of the estuary past the still-stranded English vessels. However, two of the Viking boats had suffered such casualties that they did not have the rowers to get past the coast of Sussex and make good their getaway. The bedraggled remnants of the vessels' crews were brought before King Alfred, who promptly had them hanged as pirates and brigands. There were evidently limits to Alfred's clemency.

After 896, the year the naval engagement noted above and the disbanding of the Viking army, the Chronicler made a brief entry in 897 of a couple of notable deaths and then fell silent for the year 898. Asser, too, is silent, as his account of Alfred's life ceases in 893. So the final years of the best-recorded king of England's Dark Ages pass in silence. No doubt, Alfred continued to hunt – one of his major pleasures. The work of translation continued, with the king occupied in translating the Book of Psalms. It is possible that he made his son, Edward, king of Kent and the eastern shires of Wessex, as had happened to some of his older brothers. It was good practice for taking over the kingdom, and allowed Edward to strengthen the bonds of loyalty with magnates and officers that were the key to successful rule. Alfred also, undoubtedly, spent much time in prayer. Asser says in his biography that the king wanted to devote half his waking hours to prayer and, to ensure that he did so, set about developing an elaborate timing device of six candles. When the ever-present draughts of Anglo-Saxon halls caused the candles to burn unevenly, he had lanterns made of wood and finely shaved, translucent ox horn so the candles burned steadily through day and night.

The law too, took up much of Alfred's time, as it had throughout his reign. The king was the final court of appeal and, by God's mandate, the source of justice in Anglo-Saxon England. As such, he was always on call to render judgement, a part of Alfred's life which is brought vividly to life by a letter, that survives from the reign of Alfred's son, Edward, describing a long and complicated legal case. In the letter, the writer describes bringing the case to the king:

> And the king stood in the chamber at Wardour – he was washing his hands. When he had finished, he asked Æthelhelm why what we had decided for him did not seem just to him; he [the king] said he could think of nothing more just than that he [Helmstan] should be allowed to give the oath if he could. I then said that he wished to attempt it, and asked the king to appoint a day for it, and then he did so.[7]

In a time before policemen, detectives and lawyers, Anglo-Saxon law was based on oath giving, and being able to find trustworthy men to give oath in support of you. But, from our point of view, what is fascinating is how Alfred, even when in his bedroom washing, was still expected to render judgement in a lawsuit. To be king was to be ever on show and in demand. It must have been an exhausting life.

After his silence in 898, the Chronicler had something to report towards the end of the Year of Our Lord, 899.

> In this year Alfred son of Æthelwulf died six days before All Saints' Day. He was king over the whole English people, except for that part which was under Danish rule; and he held that kingdom for twenty-eight and a half years. And then his son Edward succeeded to the kingdom.[8]

The king was dead.

11

The Once and Future King

For the man who had saved the kingdom and who had reigned for longer than any king of Wessex, the Chronicler's announcement of Alfred's death was muted. But there were other, urgent, matters for his attention in the year 900. Alfred had reigned for twenty-eight-and-a-half years and, certainly for the latter part of his reign, there were no credible internal challengers to his rule. But when an Anglo-Saxon king died, there were no clear rules on succession; whichever ætheling could command the support of the witan and gather the magnates of the kingdom to his cause would be the man who took the crown. Alfred had done his best to ensure that the ætheling would be his eldest son, Edward, by settling on him, in his will, the largest part of his land and wealth. Thus, Edward had the means to buy support, and his performance as a commander against the Viking invasions of the 890s had also served to show his ability. But there were other candidates for the crown of Wessex: the sons of Alfred's older brother,

Æthelred. Æthelred had had two sons before he died in 871, Æthelhelm and Æthelwold (yes, Æthelred kept up the family naming tradition). Born before Edward, if they had not been children on their father's death one or other of them could have claimed the throne rather than Alfred. Through Alfred's long reign, they had remained in the background, but as the king grew older, and made moves to signal that he wanted his son to succeed him, one of the two sons of Æthelred grew increasingly restive. Æthelwold was convinced his right to the throne was superior to that of Edward, and when Alfred died, he made his move.

Calling those men who were beholden to him to his side, Æthelwold seized the royal vills at Wimborne, where his father was buried, and Twyham. By taking Wimborne, Æthelwold was making a clarion call for his right to rule – he had stepped aside for Alfred, when the kingdom should have fallen to him, and waited. Now, with Alfred dead, Wessex was his due because of his patience and forbearance. Barricaded in Wimborne, Æthelwold proclaimed that he would live, or die, upon the holy ground where lay his father.

Edward did not see the matter in the same light. Bringing his forces to Badbury, near Wimborne, he prepared to storm the royal vill. However, before he could do so, Æthelwold chose to live and fight another day, stealing away with his retainers – but, the *Chronicle* reports, without his mistress, a former nun. If Æthelwold could not attract enough warriors to his side in Wessex to support his claim for the throne, he knew there were other places that would be more than happy to provide swords for an ætheling to what had become the most powerful kingdom in the country. Æthelwold fled to

Northumbria, where, according to the *Chronicle*, the Vikings of York acclaimed him king. The son of Æthelred now had a power base from which to launch his attempt to take the throne, and the Vikings had found a wedge to break the political unity of the kingdom of Wessex.

Having secured his support in York, in 902 Æthelwold attacked East Anglia, forcing the submission of the Vikings there to him. Edward, watching, knew that the test was coming for him soon too.

In 903, the storm broke. Æthelwold, ætheling of Wessex, led his Viking forces into Mercia and started ravaging the kingdom. Edward, in response, attacked Essex and East Anglia, and then withdrew. But his rearguard, led by the ealdorman of Kent, lingered and was caught by Æthelwold's returning army. In the savage battle that followed, both the ealdorman of Kent and Æthelwold himself were killed. While the Viking forces were the ones who held the field of battle, the death of Æthelwold removed the only rival to Edward's rule, for Æthelred's other son was quite content not to be king.

With unity regained in the house of Wessex, Edward, with his sister Æthelflæd and her husband Ealdorman Æthelred, the lord of the Mercians, began the slow reconquest of the Danelaw, that part of Britain that had fallen under Viking rule. Using the strategy pioneered by Alfred, Wessex and Mercia combined to put constant pressure on the Viking kingdoms, building fortified burhs to hold the land they took. When Ealdorman Æthelred suffered a debilitating illness sometime between 899 and 909, Æthelflæd took command of the Mercian half of the assault on the Danelaw, becoming known as the 'Lady of the Mercians'. Together, brother and sister pushed deeper and deeper into Viking-held territory, slowly forcing the submission of the Viking kings to their sovereignty.

Æthelflæd died on 12 June 918, having received the submission of the Vikings of York. Edward completed the process of taking the Five Boroughs of the Viking Midlands – Derby, Leicester, Stamford, Nottingham and Lincoln – and the *Chronicle* concludes its entry for the year 918 by saying, 'And all the people who had settled in Mercia, both Danish and English, submitted to him.'

Edward's son Æthelstan took the throne in 924 upon Edward's death. His father had reigned for twenty-four years, nearly matching Alfred's longevity. Æthelstan continued the expansion and consolidation wrought by his father and grandfather, adding the kingdom of Northumbria to his dominion. There was now one king ruling a territory that matches the marches of England and Æthelstan himself can legitimately be called the first king of England. Where Alfred had become, by the end of his reign, the king of the Anglo-Saxons, and Edward expanded that realm to include much of the territory previously held by the Vikings, it was Æthelstan who brought all the petty kingdoms and earldoms of the land under a single dominion. Five centuries after the Angles and the Saxons had first landed on the shores of Britain, amid the fragmentation of the unity of Rome, a single country had been created again. And chief among its architects were Alfred, his son Edward, his daughter Æthelflæd and his grandson Æthelstan. The house of Wessex had weathered the storm and created a country from the wreckage of the Viking invasions. Although the Vikings would return again, the idea of England was such that it survived even when England was, in fact, conquered, and in the end the idea conquered the conquerors.

But such was the glory that Edward the Elder, Æthelstan and his successors accrued in the tenth century that Alfred's fame waned to some extent after his death. In a culture that was still largely oral, renown rested more on the gifts of a scop than the scratchings of a chronicler. The two combined, however, in praise of Æthelstan, when the *Chronicle* records a praise poem telling of the king's victory at the Battle of Brunanburh in 937. But, in the long run, memories fade where writing, in haphazard fashion, endures. And, in particular, legends began clustering like barnacles around the time in Alfred's life which most resembled myth: his exile on the Isle of Athelney. About a hundred years after his death, the anonymous *Life of St Neot* included, for the first time in writing, the story that grew so much it has eventually all but swallowed up the name: ask what people today know of Alfred and they will answer, 'Cakes.' Given that Alfred had escaped with his household retainers, it seems unlikely that any swineherd would not have known that he had someone out of the ordinary staying in his hut – the presence of heavily armed bodyguards would have given the game away. But the way in which the story presents Alfred meekly accepting the rebuke of the swineherd's wife when he let her cakes burn suggests a compelling insight into the king's character: he took her chastisement, and the greater chastisement visited upon him by the Vikings, as being God's scourge, to bear, to understand and to amend his conduct accordingly. After the relative inaction of his first period as king, Alfred emerged from the marshes a man transformed, a man on a mission from God. Only such a commission could explain the energy and persistence he brought to the transformation of Wessex such that, when the final Viking storm broke, the kingdom could weather it relatively unscathed. And through folk tales like this, Alfred's name lived on, becoming proverbial in tale and folklore as a synonym for good governance.

However, it was not until the sixteenth century, and the Reformation, that Alfred became politically important again. As the Tudor rulers of England sought to separate themselves from the Catholic Church, Alfred slowly came to be seen as an important figure in preserving the integrity of the country against foreign invasion and influence – just as the later Tudors presented themselves. In fact, it was Elizabeth's archbishop of Canterbury, Matthew Parker, who began collecting Anglo-Saxon manuscripts that had come on the market after the Dissolution of the Monasteries. It was he who first published Asser's *Life of King Alfred* in 1574. Through the seventeenth century, a number of scholars used Alfred as the vehicle for criticising or praising the monarchy, while scholars from Oxford University cultivated the (erroneous) idea that the king had been the founder of their university – thus ensuring its priority over Cambridge.

Alfred's stock continued to rise in the eighteenth century, particularly among the nobility. Anyone wandering through the magnificent grounds of Stowe House in Buckinghamshire will find the Temple of British Worthies, a monument containing busts of sixteen men the architect, William Kent, and his client, Richard Temple, 1st Viscount Cobham, deemed most honourable in British history. Alfred was one of four monarchs and princes commemorated (the others were

Edward, the Black Prince, Elizabeth I and William III) and above his bust the inscription shows how Alfred's standing had increased through the centuries:

> The mildest, justest, most beneficent of Kings; who drove out the Danes, secur'd the Seas, protected Learning, establish'd Juries, crush'd Corruption, guarded Liberty, and was the Founder of the English Constitution.

Through the mysterious alchemy of symbols, Alfred had become the prototype of the nation and of Englishmen. As England began to project power abroad with increasing confidence, Alfred came to be seen as the source of that strength, so much so that when, in 1740, Frederick, Prince of Wales, commissioned *Alfred: a Masque*, its finale took the form of a rousing chorus announcing Britain's emergence as a major power and, by its own announcement, guarantor of freedom. 'Rule Britannia' is the finale, and Alfred, who at least did take a considerable interest in naval matters even if the results of his sea battles were rather mixed, was the man to first rule the waves and ensure Britons never will be slaves.

Through the end of the eighteenth century and on into the nineteenth, as the Napoleonic Wars raged and the threat of invasion loomed large, patriotic dramas filled the London stages, with Alfred appearing as the guarantor of English liberty. When that storm was finally spent, the nineteenth century saw the millennium of Alfred's birth as the British Empire neared its zenith of power and confidence; in such circumstances the first king of the Anglo-Saxons could hardly escape the attentions of Imperial hagiographers. In 1877, a statue to Alfred was erected in his place of birth, Wantage in Berkshire. In 1901, slightly late for the millennium of his death, another statue of Alfred was installed in Winchester. The stream of books that had flowed from the printing presses about Alfred during the nineteenth century slowed somewhat after the carnage of the First World War, when the imperial project lost its lustre in the mud of the Somme, but through the decades since there has been a steady stream of books and articles, many of the more recent bemoaning the diminution of Alfred into the king who burned the cakes. But with the excitement of the possible location of some of Alfred's remains, and the ongoing hope that more might be located, I hope that Alfred's stock will rise again, stripped free from propaganda and simply looking at the extraordinary life and deeds of the first king of the Anglo-Saxons, and the only king in English history to be called 'the Great'.

12

The Post-Mortem Story of Alfred

Dr Katie Tucker

The story of the post-mortem fate of Alfred's remains is a long and complicated one, with the king never being permitted to rest in peace for very long. Upon his death, he was first buried in the Old Minster, in a tomb of precious porphyry marble.[1] However, William of Malmesbury and the *Liber Monasterii de Hyda* both report that the canons were convinced that Alfred's spirit 'resumed his corpse' and went wandering around the buildings of the church.[2] Therefore, when the New Minster was completed in 903, his son Edward the Elder had the 'bones' and 'ashes' of his father moved to a chapel within the new building.[3] When Alfred's wife, Ealhswith, died shortly afterwards, she was also buried in the New Minster,[4] and when Edward died in 924, his body was also laid to rest there, on the right side of the altar.[5] It is also recorded that Edward's brother, Æthelweard, who had died four years before Edward, as well as a son of Edward, also called Æthelweard (and otherwise known as Ælfweard), who died a few days after his father, were buried there,[6] with the only other royal burial specifically mentioned as taking place at New Minster being that of King Eadwig, who died in 959.[7] It has previously been accepted that one of the wives of Edward, Ælfflæd, as well as two of his daughters, Eadflæd and Eadhild, were also buried in New Minster,[8] as they were described in the English translation of William of Malmesbury, by Giles, as having been buried close to each other at Winchester.[9] However, this would appear to be a mistranslation, as the original Latin text says they were buried at Wilton, 'Wiltonaie', not Winchester, 'Wyntoniae'.[10] Eadburh, another daughter of Edward, described by William of Malmesbury as being buried at an unspecified location in Winchester, is recorded elsewhere as being buried at Nunnaminster.[11]

The remains of Alfred, Edward, Ealhswith and the other members of the royal family were then only permitted to rest in peace for another two hundred years. The buildings of the Old and New Minsters (the Old Minster later to be replaced by the present cathedral) were so close together that the choirs were reported to be able to hear each other's singing, the church bells tolling in different keys made a terrible noise, and the ground around the New Minster became so boggy and fetid that it became intolerable for the monks to continue to inhabit the place.[12] In the early eleventh century, Henry I gave the monks of New Minster some land outside the northern gate of the medieval city on which to build a new monastery,[13] and in 1110, the New Minster was translated there 'with the monks and relics'[14] and renamed Hyde Abbey. The relics that were moved included the bones of Saint Judoc, a seventh-century Breton, whose relics were installed in New Minster upon its foundation[15] (although it has also been suggested that his relics were not translated to Hyde[16]), the head of St Valentine, which had been given to New Minster in 1041 by Queen Ælfgifu,[17] and the body of the monk Grimbald, a close associate of Alfred, which had been kept there in a silver shrine.[18]

There are no contemporary sources that refer to the bodies of the Wessex royal family being moved from the site of New Minster to Hyde, and while many nineteenth-century and later commentators have referred to the bodies being transported across Winchester in a splendid procession accompanied by palm branches, this appears to be a conflation of the translation to Hyde with the instructions for joint Easter processions between the monks of the newly founded Hyde Abbey and the cathedral, contained in an early twelfth-century document.[19] However, it is probably safe to assume that when New Minster was dissolved, the buildings demolished and the land given to the new cathedral, the bodies were translated to the new monastery, as was the case for a number of Saxon royals who were moved from Old Minster to the crypt of the new cathedral in the late eleventh century.[20]

The first reference to the remains having been moved to Hyde comes from Leland, writing shortly after the Dissolution of the Monasteries, who stated that 'the bones of Alfredus ... and of Edward his sunne and king, were translatid from Newanminstre, and layid in a tumbe before the high altare at Hyde'.[21] Leland does not mention the location of the grave of Ealhswith, or of any of the other royals, possibly suggesting that they were not in a prominent place within the church. It is probably safe to assume that the graves then remained undisturbed until the 1530s, as, although the buildings of Hyde Abbey were very badly damaged in the fire that occurred as part of the 1141 'Rout of Winchester' during the Anarchy,[22] with Bowker stating that the tomb of Alfred was also damaged,[23] there does not appear to be any reference to this in contemporary sources.

In 1538, the monastery of Hyde was dissolved, with Thomas Wriothesley describing how they were intending to 'sweep away all the rotten bones that be called relics'.[24] It seems likely that this included the remains of Grimbald, St Judoc (if his relics had been moved to Hyde in the first place) and St Valentine, although probably not those of Alfred, Edward and Ealhswith. Writing in 1901, Thomas Hughes relates the story, unfortunately without reference to earlier sources, that Dr Richard Fox, the bishop of Winchester, had the remains of the royal burials – including those from Hyde, which had been disturbed at the Dissolution – collected into lead chests and placed around the presbytery in the cathedral.[25] They remained there until 1642, when Parliamentarian troops broke open the chests and scattered the contents, with the bones subsequently being collected and taken to Oxford, where they were 'lodged in a repository building next the public library'.[26] This is probably a misunderstanding by Hughes of the work carried out by Fox in 1524 to rehouse the bones of a number of Anglo-Saxon kings and bishops that had previously been moved from the cathedral crypt in the twelfth century to a place known as the 'Holy Hole' behind the high altar.[27] The mortuary chests that Fox commissioned are still extant, with the names of their original occupants painted on the outer wooden cases. None of the individuals assumed to have been moved to Hyde are included, suggesting that their bodies were not amongst those rehoused in this way, although interestingly, it is known that there were originally at least two, and possibly four, more chests than now survive. It has been suggested that this was because four of the chests were destroyed in 1642 with the remains being gathered up into two new chests,[28] but there is the slight possibility that two of the chests were indeed removed and taken to Oxford, although if this was the case, it is not known what became of them. Whether or not there is any truth in this story, it is known that the graves of Alfred and Edward were opened at the time of the Dissolution or shortly before, as Leland reports that '2. litle tables of leade inscribid with theyr names' were found in the tomb.[29] However, it is not known to what extent the burials were disturbed.

The next time we hear of the graves, it is in 1788, when the land upon which Hyde Abbey stood was sold off for the building of the new County Bridewell. Henry Howard, who was quartered with the military in Winchester in 1797, met with the keeper of the Bridewell, Mr Page, and communicated his findings about what had happened to the burials to the Society of Antiquaries of London the following year.[30] He stated that in one place, within the east end of the church, a stone coffin was found 'cased with lead both within and without, and containing some bones and remains of garments'.[31] The lead from the coffin was sold 'for two guineas', the 'bones were thrown about', and the 'stone coffin broken into pieces'.[32] He also stated that there were 'two other coffins, and no more, found in this part', which were also broken up and buried 'as low as the spring'.[33] A number of other coffins were found further west, in the presumed nave of the church, as well as further to the east and south, outside of the beaten clay foundation that was taken to denote the extent of the building. Although it is explicitly stated that the stone coffins were reburied 'for the sake of the garden',[34] it is not known what happened to the bones that had been removed from the coffins and 'thrown about', but presumably a number of them were also reburied in the course of the works, even if this was not done as a deliberate act. The historian John Milner also wrote about the building of the Bridewell after having witnessed that 'at almost every stroke of the mattock or spade, some ancient sepulcher was violated', with the contents being treated with 'marked indignity', and that a great number of stone coffins were found, as well as chalices, patens, rings, buckles, leather, velvet and gold lace and parts of a crosier.[35]

The next part of the story takes place in early 1867, when a disgruntled correspondent, calling himself 'Q', writes to the *Hampshire Chronicle* to report on a 'scandalous indecency' that 'is now in course of perpetration in the City of Winchester'.[36] He states that a 'so-called antiquarian' has been making excavations on the land formally occupied by Hyde Abbey and has 'dug up the remains of the dead deposited many centuries ago in ground consecrated and supposed inviolable' (he had obviously not taken into account the destruction of burials that had taken place on the site only eighty years previously), with 'several skulls and numerous leg and arm bones, vertebrae etc. lying huddled together in a candle-box' while 'the skeleton of another corpse lies exposed by the side of a chalk vault, from which it has been lifted piecemeal'. This antiquarian was named John Mellor and he was swift to reply to the allegations made about his 'researches'.[37] He stated that he was anxious to discover the remains of King Alfred and set to work with a 'feeling of reverence for the "mighty dead"', and was successful in his endeavours, having found the remains of several persons, including the king and also the burial vault of Edward, with the remains of a sceptre, gilt cloth and various other items. He also writes that he removed the bones 'in simple faith, with reverence and deep respect' to save them from 'further mutilation and violence'. A letter in the same edition of the paper, written by Hugh Wyeth, one of the churchwardens of Hyde parish church, St Bartholomew's, states that the vicar, William Williams, requested him to take charge of all the remains, and this he did, with Mellor 'most willingly plac[ing] at my disposal the whole of the skeletons'. The remains were placed into two boxes and taken to the parish church, where the intention was to have a plain oak mortuary chest made for them and for them to be deposited in a niche within the church upon its rebuilding.

However, the story did not end there, with 'Q' again writing to the *Chronicle* to divulge extra details about Mellor's conduct, including that he had offered portions of the remains for sale to at least two householders, with a servant of one of them 'incautiously' accepting them, only for them to be 'thrown by a disgruntled housemaid into the dust bin' the following morning.[38] Mellor then again responded to the allegations, saying that he knew nothing of these stories, but that he had been refused permission to deposit the remains at the museum, so had been allowed by a 'medical gentleman at the hospital' to place the remains in the exhibition rooms until he had obtained a new case to put them in. He concluded his letter by stating that he was about to leave Winchester and therefore would not be able to reply to any further observations.[39]

In 1871, Mellor published a pamphlet that gave much greater detail about his work at Hyde Abbey.[40] In it, he claimed to have found the bodies of Alfred, Edward, Æthelweard, Ealhswith and Queen Ælfgifu in the choir, with a 'silver sceptre, a plate of lead with the king's name upon it, silver coins, gilt cloth, ermine, and embers from the fire of 1141',[41] with, coincidently, this discovery taking place on the anniversary of Alfred's death.[42] He also said that the bodies of Alfred, Ealhswith and Æthelweard were still within the three stone coffins that Howard had reported as being found in 1788, with Edward and his wife being found in a 'chalk vault to the left of the stone coffins',[43] although he then also goes on to contradict himself by writing that Mr Page had told Henry Howard that in 1788, once he had recognised the remains as those of royalty, he had left them alone, 'coffinless', at the bottom of the burial vault.[44] In the course of his work, Mellor also claimed to have found the 'withered and much-dried severed and venerable head' of St Valentine, at the foot of the altar steps.[45]

Mellor's research was much criticised by other commentators, with his honesty being brought into question over exactly what he had found. These included claims that he had found a battleaxe on the site that was shown to have been lying around the yard of a local blacksmith's for some time and had been thrown on to the site by persons unknown for him to find, and also that he had said he had found a Roman coin that had obviously been dug up quite a long time before his work at Hyde.[46]. More importantly, the lead plates that he claimed to have found in the vault along with the remains of Alfred, Æthelweard and Ealhswith were clearly of modern manufacture and were only produced by Mellor upon the vault being backfilled.[47]

Once the remains had been handed over to the parish church, they were photographed, with the curate, John Wright, writing a small piece for *The Gentleman's Magazine*, with engravings of the photographs being included.[48] These showed five crania (skulls) in varying states of completeness and preservation, with the most complete also having its mandible present. The remains were then reburied, according to a letter in the Hampshire Record Office, probably written by Madeleine, the daughter of Hugh Wyeth[49] in a grave outside the east end of the church, with a cross but no inscription being carved upon it. Mellor also confirmed this is where the remains were placed, describing them as being reburied in a small brick vault, covered with a plain stone slab.[50] This is where the bones remained until the first phase of the new project finally began, in March 2013.

13

The Unmarked Grave and the Search for Alfred
Dr Katie Tucker

It was on a very cold and windy morning in March 2013 that the project that had been the culmination of years of intentions and months of detailed planning was finally to begin. As part of the celebrations organised in 2010 by Hyde900, a community group set up to commemorate the 900th anniversary of the founding of Hyde Abbey, with the support of St Bartholomew's church and involvement from the University of Winchester, the decision had been made that the time had come to try and investigate the contents of the vault (known as the Unmarked Grave) outside the east end of St Bartholomew's, where it was supposed that the remains excavated by John Mellor from Hyde Abbey, and now popularly assumed to include the remains of King Alfred, had been reburied in the final third of the nineteenth century. A long and complicated process followed to obtain a 'faculty permission' from the Diocesan Chancellor (required as the bones were in consecrated ground) to open the grave and investigate the contents. Following a media furore about the new project in February 2013,[1] partially fuelled by the announcement the previous day by the University of Leicester that they had successfully identified the remains of Richard III,[2] and with concerns over the security of the grave, an emergency petition was granted allowing the excavation of the grave to take place.

The excavation, led by the author and supported by colleagues from the University of Winchester, began with the lifting of the ledger slab from the top of the grave, underneath which was a small rectangular vault formed by a single thickness of red bricks, much as described by Mellor in 1871.[3] The grave also appeared to be completely full of soil and the next task was to remove this, which we started to do. However, after digging down only three courses of brick, we found, rather than the grave being completely full of soil, that it was sealed by two further slabs laid next to one another and bricked into place. Through the narrow gap between the slabs, it was possible to see a number of human bones, including femorae, humeri, tibiae, vertebrae, ribs and parts of the pelvis, lying on the bottom of the vault. Once one of these slabs was removed, it could be seen that there were a large number of long bones and parts of the pelvis in the centre of the vault, with a pile of smaller bones to the east end, and five crania placed carefully at the west end, exactly the number that had been photographed in the nineteenth century. It therefore certainly seemed likely that these were the bones excavated by Mellor, but could Alfred, Edward, Æthelweard and Ealhswith be among them?

The bones were carefully removed from the vault and taken back to the University of Winchester for safe storage, but it wasn't until August 2013 that the second part of the faculty permission, to analyse and date the bones, was granted. The osteological analysis, undertaken by the author, revealed that there were parts of six separate skeletons, as well as a few bones that could not be associated with a particular individual, represented among the remains removed from the vault. These comprised the largely complete skeleton of a female in her mid-twenties to mid-thirties, with evidence for a chronic infectious lung or digestive disease that had also affected most of the skeleton; the largely complete skeleton of a possible male in their forties, with evidence for arthritis, as well as ankylosing spondylitis and DISH (diffuse idiopathic skeletal hyperostosis), two conditions that lead to fusion of the spine, ribcage and pelvis, with subsequent loss of movement; the largely complete skeleton of a male in their mid-thirties to mid-forties, also with evidence for arthritis and early-stage DISH; the less complete skeleton of a probable male in their mid-thirties to mid-forties, with evidence for Paget's disease, a condition that leads to thickening and weakening of bone; and two largely incomplete skeletons of adults, represented by only a few bones. It was also possible to compare the five crania excavated from the Unmarked Grave with those photographed in the nineteenth century to show that they were indeed the same ones that Mellor had found at Hyde Abbey and handed over to St Bartholomew's in 1867.

The osteological analysis did not contradict the possibility that members of the Wessex royal family were among the remains, as Alfred and Edward were both thought to have died in their late forties, with Alfred's son, Æthelweard, probably being in his early forties. However, for individuals that had been exhumed and reburied at least once (at least twice in the case of Alfred) and also disturbed at least once since then, the remains, at least of three of the individuals, seemed to be too well preserved and too complete, with even very small, fragile bones being present. The only way to determine if there was still a chance that any of the bones could belong to Alfred or his family was to take samples for radiocarbon dating. Alfred had died in 899, Ealhswith in 903, Æthelweard in 920, Edward and his son Æthelweard in 924 and Eadwig in 959, while Hyde Abbey was founded in 1110, with any burials associated with the abbey having to have been made after this date, so there was enough of a gap between these events for radiocarbon analysis to be able to distinguish between them. The radiocarbon dating was undertaken by Oxford University's Radiocarbon Accelerator Unit (ORAU), with samples being taken from each of the five crania and a long bone from each of the post-cranial skeletons. It was then a waiting game while the samples were processed and the dates obtained but when the results came in, they were disappointing but not unexpected. All of the remains dated to the period around the founding of Hyde Abbey or later, with dates ranging from around 1030–1150 for the oldest individual (one of the very incomplete skeletons) to around 1415–1460 for the latest (the individual with ankylosing spondylitis and DISH). Therefore, while the remains belonged to a very interesting small group of individuals with a number of unusual pathologies, there was no chance that any of the remains could belong to members of the Wessex royal family and it seemed like that was the end of the story.

However, in the 1990s, there had been an excavation at the site of Hyde Abbey by Winchester Museums Service and Earthwatch, part of which focused on the post-Dissolution activity at the east end of the abbey church.[4] I knew that they had found part of an adult female pelvis that had been radiocarbon dated to the post-medieval period and, despite the reports at the time that said this was the only piece of human bone found,[5] this seemed unlikely. I thought it was worth investigating further, to see if this was indeed the case, or whether there was more bone from the east end of the abbey that could be analysed and dated as part of the new project. I therefore contacted the Museums Service to be told that, yes, there was more human bone, two boxes of it, that had only been identified as human sometime after the end of their project, when there was no more money for any further radiocarbon dates, especially when the one sample they did have analysed had produced such a late date. They were very happy for me to look at the material and have more samples taken for radiocarbon analysis.

The first step was to identify exactly where all of the bone came from. As well as the east end of the abbey church, the excavation had also investigated parts of the cemetery outside the south wall of the building, with the majority of the bone in the two boxes coming from that area and therefore not being of relevance. However, what was of relevance to the story was that the excavation had revealed evidence that a number of the graves in the cemetery had been opened and 'rifled' in the eighteenth or nineteenth century, with chalk slabs from the tops of graves being moved and bones being left in disarray. This seemed to be evidence for the activities that had been reported as taking place during the building of the Bridewell in 1788, with John Milner reporting that a great number of stone coffins had been dug up and their contents 'treated with marked indignity',[6] as well as when John Mellor was digging at the site during 1866 and 1867 and leaving skeletons 'exposed by the side of ... chalk vault[s]'.[7] Therefore, the written reports of the time seemed to be telling the truth about what had taken place.

The excavation also found evidence for three pits having been dug in the area where the high altar was presumed to have stood. The earliest of these was a large circular pit that extended across nearly the full width of the building and was located almost exactly where Henry Howard had marked the three stone coffins as having been found in his report of 1798.[8] In the edges of this pit it was also possible to see the remains of three earlier grave pits and there were broken-up pieces of stone at the base of the pit that may have been from sarcophagi. It therefore seemed certain that this was the pit dug by the prisoners in 1788. To the south of this pit and cutting away part of it was a much smaller rectangular pit that extended to the edge of the south wall of the church. It is very likely that this is the pit dug by John Mellor in 1866 and it seems that he was digging in the wrong place to have rediscovered the remains of Alfred and his family that he claims had been reburied by Mr Page in 1788.[9] This is confirmed by the plan included by Mellor in his 1871 publication, which shows four graves in the south part of the east end of the church that he claimed were those of Alfred, Ealhswith, Edward (with his wife Ecgwynn) and Æthelweard,[10] exactly in the location of the pit found in the 1990s excavation. Mellor's plan also included the location of what he believed to be Grimbald's grave, which he indicated as being represented by two rectangular pits to the north and slightly west of the four graves. This corresponds almost exactly with the location of two graves found in the 1990s excavation that had been emptied in the eighteenth or nineteenth century. It therefore seems very probable that at least some of the bones we had excavated from the Unmarked Grave and which had been dated to the period of the use of Hyde Abbey came from these six graves and are likely to have belonged to important members of the religious community or wealthy patrons of the abbey. The latest pit in the area of the high altar was to the east of the Mellor pit, cutting away a small part of the eastern edge of it as well as part of the southern extent of the 1788 pit. This pit was large and rectangular and extended out past the eastern edge of the 1990s excavation trench, with part of it also being found in another trench dug during the 1990s excavation to the east of the area of the high altar. This seems to correspond to the trench dug by Alfred Bowker in the 1890s that he recorded as having contained a 'portion of wall, proving that the eastern end of the abbey was apsidal in shape and some distance to the east of where Mr Howard and others took the east to be'.[11] However, rather than assuming that this meant the diggings of 1788 had been in the wrong place to find the graves of Alfred and his family, it rather suggests that Bowker had found the outer wall of the ambulatory to the east of the high altar and the ambulatory chapel, parts of which were also uncovered in the 1990s excavation. The major question was, had any bones from the original graves of Alfred, Edward and Ealhswith survived these successive acts of disturbance?

I identified six contexts, either from within the three pits or from the immediate surroundings, where human bone had been found. Henry Howard's report on the diggings of 1788 stated that the bones had been 'thrown about',[12] so it was probable that most of them would not have remained within the confines of the pit and, even if they had, both Mellor and Bowker had disturbed this pit in the course of their investigations. The bone within these contexts was analysed and included two parts of an adult humerus (upper arm bone), one part of which was from the 1788 pit and one part from a pit to the west of what Mellor had described as Grimbald's grave; parts of an adult female skull and some ribs and vertebrae from a pit that cut through the north wall of the church; part of an adult male skull and some long bones from two separate contexts within a pit in the southern ambulatory; and part of an adult male pelvis from within John Mellor's pit. Samples from all of these were then sent off for radiocarbon dating, again at Oxford, and then began another wait for the results.

When they finally came back, all but one of the samples proved to be in the same date range as the individuals from the Unmarked Grave, with the female skull returning a date of 1021–1155 and thereby tying in very well with the foundation of the abbey, and with the other samples being dated to the thirteenth to fifteenth centuries. However, one sample, taken from the adult male pelvis, came back with a date of 895–1017. This was much too early to be from a primary burial made at Hyde Abbey and there was no evidence from previous excavations that the site had been used for burial before the abbey was founded, with the charter of 983, in which Aethelred gave part of the land to New Minster (the rest being given to Henry I), specifically stating that it was a water-meadow.[13] Therefore, the only explanation seemed to be that the bone was from one of the individuals moved to Hyde Abbey from New Minster in 1110 but the radiocarbon date range encompassed the death dates of Alfred, Edward, Edward's brother, Æthelweard, and his son of the same name, as well as Eadwig and Grimbald. So, was it possible to say which, if any, of these individuals the bone belonged to? The bone was from an adult in their mid-twenties to mid-forties, which would discount Edward's son, Æthelweard, who died at the age of twenty-one or twenty-two, Eadwig, who was probably in his late teens or early twenties, and also Grimbald, who died in his eighties (although it also seems very probable that Grimbald's remains, which had been housed in a silver shrine at New Minster and subsequently at Hyde Abbey, were destroyed along with the other relics, including those of St Valentine and St Judoc, at the Dissolution). However, the ages at death of Alfred, Edward and his brother Æthelweard would all be consistent, as, even though both Alfred and Edward were probably in their very late forties or early fifties, the osteological methods used to determine an age from the pelvis tend to underage older individuals, meaning an upper age limit of mid-forties for the piece of bone is only to be taken as a guide. The only other pieces of evidence that could be used to suggest a possible identity for the bone are the statements of Leland and Howard about the graves in front of the high altar, with Leland only specifically referring to Alfred and Edward, while Howard states that only three coffins were found, presumably those of Alfred, Ealhswith and Edward.[14]

Without any evidence for where the grave of Æthelweard was located in the abbey church, it can be argued that the bone is more likely to belong to Edward or to Alfred, and therefore, ironically, John Mellor may have actually found what he was digging for but thrown it back, unrecognised.

So where could we go from here? The fact that only one piece of bone with the correct date was identified during the research meant that it would have been possible to take a sample for DNA analysis but there would have been nothing to compare it to. A few years ago, the remains of Alfred's granddaughter, Eadgyth, were identified in a tomb within the cathedral at Magdeburg, Germany, but, unfortunately, it was not possible to retrieve viable DNA from her remains.[15] However, new research on the mortuary chests containing the remains of Saxon kings and bishops at the cathedral in Winchester includes DNA analysis on the remains[16] and, as one of those supposedly housed in the chests is Alfred's father, Æthelwulf,[17] there is now the possibility that DNA comparisons between the remains in the chests and the piece of bone from Hyde Abbey could take place at some point in the future. A serious plan for a re-excavation at the site of the east end of the church has also been proposed, in order to re-investigate the base of the 1788 pit (excavation of which was completed in the 1990s but hampered by ground water) and to investigate the full extent of Alfred Bowker's 1890s trench, only parts of which were re-excavated in the 1990s. It is hoped that this can take place in 2015 and, with the possibility of finding more fragments of bone, it seems that the story of Alfred is not yet over.

Notes

1 The King at Bay

1. Colgrave, Bertram (1985). *Felix's Life of Saint Guthlac*. Cambridge University Press (Cambridge), p. 87
2. Keynes, Simon and Lapidge, Michael (trans) (2004). *Alfred the Great: Asser's* Life of King Alfred *and Other Contemporary Sources*. Penguin (London), p. 132.
3. *Ibid.*, p. 84.

2 The Boy Born Not to Be King

1. Keynes, Simon and Lapidge, Michael (trans) (2004). *Alfred the Great: Asser's* Life of King Alfred *and Other Contemporary Sources*. Penguin (London), p. 71.
2. *Ibid.*, p. 72.
3. *Ibid.*
4. *Ibid.*, p. 68.

5. *Ibid.*, p. 75.

6. Ingram, Revd James (trans.) (1912). *The Anglo-Saxon Chronicle.* Everyman Press (London).

7. Ingram, 851.

8. Bede (1990). *Ecclesiastical History of the English People.* Penguin (London).

9. Keynes and Lapidge, p. 69.

10. *Ibid.*, p. 232.

11. *Ibid.*, p. 70.

12. Sedgefield, Walter (1900). *King Alfred's Version of the Consolations of Boethius: Done into Modern English.*

13. Keynes and Lapidge, p. 174.

14. *Ibid.*, p. 73.

3 The Invaders Invaded

1. Keynes, Simon and Lapidge, Michael (trans) (2004). *Alfred the Great: Asser's* Life of King Alfred *and Other Contemporary Sources.* Penguin (London), p. 73.

2. Nelson, Janet L. (2004). 'Æthelwulf (*d.* 858)', *Oxford Dictionary of National Biography.* Oxford University Press (Oxford).

3. *Ibid.*

4. Keynes & Lapidge, p. 174.

5. *Ibid.*

6. Ingram, Revd James (trans.) (1912). *The Anglo-Saxon Chronicle.* Everyman Press (London).

7. Keynes and Lapidge, p. 74.

8. Whitelock, Dorothy (1979). *English Historical Documents; Volume 1, 500–1041.* Eyre & Spottiswode (London), p. 842.

9. Keynes and Lapidge, p. 99.

10. Keynes and Lapidge, p. 77.

11. Ingram.

12. *Ibid.*

13. Sweet, Henry (ed.) and Kenneth Cutler (trans.) (1961). 'The Martyrdom of St Edmund, King of East Anglia' in *Anglo-Saxon Primer*. Clarendon Press (Oxford).

14. *Ibid.*

4 The Year of Battles

1 Keynes, Simon and Lapidge, Michael (trans) (2004). *Alfred the Great: Asser's* Life of King Alfred *and Other Contemporary Sources*. Penguin (London), p. 78.

2. *Ibid.*

3. *Ibid.*, p. 79.

4. *Ibid.*

5. *Ibid.*, pp. 132–133.

6. *Ibid.*, p. 80.

5 Buying Time

1. Sturdy, David (1995). *Alfred the Great*. Constable (London), p. 127.

2. Biddle, M. and Kjølbye-Biddle, B. (1992). 'Repton and the Vikings', in *Antiquity: A Quarterly Review of Archaeology*. Volume 66, Number 250, pp. 36–51.

3. Whitelock, Dorothy (1979). *English Historical Documents; Volume 1, 500–1041*. Eyre & Spottiswode (London), p. 194.

6 To Kill a King

1. Keynes, Simon and Lapidge, Michael (trans) (2004).
   Alfred the Great: Asser's Life of King Alfred *and Other
   Contemporary Sources*. Penguin (London), p. 81.
2. Whitelock, Dorothy (1979). *English Historical Documents;
   Volume 1, 500–1041*. Eyre & Spottiswode (London), p. 542.

7 Out of the Marshes

1. Keynes, Simon and Lapidge, Michael (trans) (2004).
   Alfred the Great: Asser's Life of King Alfred *and Other
   Contemporary Sources*. Penguin (London), p. 84.
2. *Ibid.*
3. *Ibid.*, p. 85.
4. *Ibid.*
5. *Ibid.*, p. 171.

8 Rebuilding

1. Alexander, Michael (1977). *The Earliest English Poems*.
   Penguin (Harmondsworth), p. 107.
2. *Ibid.*
3. Keynes, Simon and Lapidge, Michael (trans) (2004).
   Alfred the Great: Asser's Life of King Alfred *and Other
   Contemporary Sources*. Penguin (London), pp. 124–125.
4. Brooks, Nicholas (1984). *The Early History of the Church
   of Canterbury*. Leicester University Press (Leicester), pp.
   172–173.
5. Keynes and Lapidge, p. 99.

6. *Ibid.*, p. 126.

7. *Ibid.*

8. *Ibid.*

9. *Ibid.*, p. 132.

10. *Ibid.*, p. 126.

11. *Ibid.*, p. 148.

12. *Ibid.*, p. 90

13. *Ibid.*, p. 93.

14. *Ibid.*

15. *Ibid.*

16. *Ibid.*, p. 97.

17. *Ibid.*, p. 105.

18. *Ibid.*, p. 183.

19. *Ibid.*, pp. 113–114.

9 Landhold

1. Keynes, Simon and Lapidge, Michael (trans) (2004). *Alfred the Great: Asser's* Life of King Alfred *and Other Contemporary Sources*. Penguin (London), p. 96.

2. *Ibid.*, pp. 97–98.

3. Bede (1990). *Ecclesiastical History of the English People*. Penguin (London), pp. 107–108.

4. Sturdy, David (1995). *Alfred the Great*. Constable (London), p. 176.

5. *Ibid.*, p. 201.

6. Robertson, A. J. (1956). *Anglo-Saxon Charters*. Cambridge University Press (Cambridge), pp. 496–496.

10 Back to the Barricades

1. Abels, Richard (1988). *Lordship and Military Obligation in Anglo-Saxon England*. British Museum Publications (London), p. 285.
2. Bately, Janet (ed.) (1980). *The Old English Orosius*. Oxford University Press (Oxford), p. 83.
3. Sturdy, David (1995). *Alfred the Great*. Constable (London), p. 174.
4. *Ibid.*, p. 175.
5. *Ibid.*, p. 204.
6. Keynes, Simon and Lapidge, Michael (trans) (2004). *Alfred the Great: Asser's* Life of King Alfred *and Other Contemporary Sources*. Penguin (London), p. 118.
7. Abels, p. 280.
8. *Ibid.*, p. 120.

12 The Post-Mortem Story of Alfred

1. Stevenson, W. H. (ed.) (1904). *Asser's Life of King Alfred, together with the Annals of Saint Neots*. Clarendon Press (Oxford), p. 147.
2. Giles, J. A. (1847). *William of Malmesbury's Chronicle of the Kings of England*. Henry G. Bohn (London), p. 121; Edwards, E. (ed.) (1866). *Liber Monasterii de Hyda*. Longmans (London), 76.
3. De Gray Birch, W. (ed.) (1892). *Liber Vitae: Register and Martyrology of New Minster and Hyde Abbey, Winchester*. Simpkin and Co. (London), p. 5; Edwards, p. 76.

4. Edwards, p. 83.

5. De Gray Birch, p. 6.

6. Giles, p. 128.

7. *Ibid.*, p. 147.

8. See, for example, Milner (1809), pp. 225–226; and Bogan, P. (1986). 'Where is King Alfred Buried?', *Winchester Cathedral Record 55*, p. 27, although he wrongly states that Ælfflæd was Edward's daughter.

9. Giles, p. 124.

10. Hardy, T. D. (1840). *Willelmi Malmesbiriensis Monachi, Gesta Regum Anglorum*. Sumptibus Societatis (London), pp. 197–8.

11. Giles, p. 125; Edwards, p. 113.

12. Gibson, E. (1722). *Britannia, or a Chorographical Description of Great Britain and Ireland, Together with the Adjacent Islands. Written in Latin by William Camden and Translated into English, with Additions and Improvements.* Awnsham Churchill (London), p. 142.

13. Gibson, p. 142.

14. Luard, H. R. (ed.) (1865). *Annales Monastici vol. II.* Longmans (London), p. 43.

15. De Gray Birch, p. 6; Edwards, p. 82.

16. Thomas, I. G. (1974). *The Cult of Saints' Relics in Medieval England.* PhD thesis (University of London), p. 189.

17. Thorpe, B. (ed.) (1861). *The Anglo-Saxon Chronicle Vol. II: Translation.* Longmans (London), p. 132.

18. Grierson, P. (1940). 'Grimbald of St. Bertin's', *English Historical Review 220*, p. 558.

19. Dodsworth, R. and Dugdale, G. (1655). *Monasticon*

Anglicanum Vol. I. Hodgkinson (London), pp. 211–212.

20. Crook, J. (2000). *The Architectural Setting of the Cult of Saints in the early Christian West.* Oxford University Press (Oxford), pp. 219–221.

21. Smith, L. T. (1907). *The Itinerary of John Leland.* George Bell (London), p. 272.

22. Forester, T. (ed.) (1854). *The Chronicle of Florence of Worcester with the Two Continuations.* Henry Bohn (London), p. 283.

23. Bowker, A. (1902). *The King Alfred Millenary: A Record of the Proceedings of the National Commemoration.* Macmillan (London), p. 65.

24. *Ibid.,* pp. 65–66.

25. Hughes, T. (1901). *Alfred the Great.* Macmillan (London), p. 302.

26. *Ibid.,* p. 303.

27. See Milner (1820), pp. 89–90; Crook.

28. Church Monuments Society. 'Notes and Queries about the Mortuary Chests'.

29. Smith, p. 283.

30. Howard, H. (1800). 'Enquiries Concerning the Tomb of King Alfred, at Hyde Abbey, near Winchester', *Archaeologia* 13 (1800).

31. *Ibid.,* p. 311.

32. *Ibid.*

33. *Ibid.*

34. *Ibid.*

35. Milner (1820), p. 238.

36. *Hampshire Chronicle,* 11 January 1867.

37. *Hampshire Chronicle,* 19 January 1867.

38. *Hampshire Chronicle*, 26 January 1867.

39. *Hampshire Chronicle*, 2 February 1867.

40. Mellor, J. (1871). *The Curious Particulars Related to King Alfred's Death and Burial Never Before Made Public.* James Gibbs (Canterbury).

41. *Ibid.*, p. 15.

42. *Ibid.*

43. *Ibid.*, pp. 15–16.

44. *Ibid.*, p. 16.

45. Mellor, p. 11.

46. Collier, C. (1870). 'Report of Committee Appointed to Enquire into the Reputed Discoveries at Hyde', *Proceedings of the Winchester and Hampshire Scientific and Literary Society* 1, p. 22.

47. Collier, p. 23; Wright, J. P. (1968). 'Remarkable Skulls', *The Gentleman's Magazine* 225.

48. Wright.

49. HRO Ref. 94M85W/1.

50. Mellor, p. 16.

13 The Unmarked Grave and the Search for Alfred

1. See, for example, Silverman, R. (2013). 'After Richard III, Archaeologists Set Their Sights on Alfred the Great'. *The Telegraph*, 5 February 2013; Whipple, T. (2013). 'Alfred the Great Next in Line to Be Dug Up', *The Times*, 5 February 2013.

2. BBC (2013). 'Richard III Dig: DNA Confirms Bones are King's'. *BBC News*, 4 February 2013.

3. Mellor, J. (1871). *The Curious Particulars Related to King*

Alfred's Death and Burial Never Before Made Public. James Gibbs (Canterbury), p. 19.

4. Scobie, G. S. 'Report on the Excavations at Hyde Abbey, 1995–9'. Winchester Museums Archive: HA 95–99; and forthcoming.

5. See, for example, Kennedy, M. (1999). 'Riddle of Alfred's Bones'. *The Guardian,* 27 October 1999.

6. Milner (1820), p. 238.

7. *Hampshire Chronicle,* 11 January 1867.

8. Howard, H. (1800). 'Enquiries Concerning the Tomb of King Alfred, at Hyde Abbey, near Winchester', *Archaeologia* 13 (1800).

9. Mellor, p. 16.

10. *Ibid.,* p. 6.

11. Bowker, A. (1902). *The King Alfred Millenary: A Record of the Proceedings of the National Commemoration.* Macmillan (London), p. 67.

12. Howard, p. 311.

13. Charter of Aethelred S845 (Edwards, E. (ed.) (1866). *Liber Monasterii de Hyda.* Longmans (London), pp. 228–231).

14. Howard, p. 311.

15. University of Bristol (2010). 'Bones Confirmed as those of Saxon Princess Eadgyth'. *University of Bristol,* 17 June 2010.

16. Southern Daily Echo (2014). 'DNA Tests Begin on Bones of "King Canute"'. *Southern Daily Echo,* 17 April 2014.

17. Church Monuments Society. 'Notes and Queries about the Mortuary Chests'.

List of Illustrations

Map of Alfred's England. (Courtesy of David Horspool)
Alfred's family and genealogy. (Courtesy of David Horspool)

Plate Section

1. The Alfred Jewel, found near Athelney in 1693, back, front
   and side views. The legend round the side reads 'AELFRED
   MEC HEHT GEWYRCAN' – 'Alfred ordered me to be made'.
   (Courtesy of Jonathan Reeve, JRb39fp671b 800900)
2. The ring of King Ælthelwulf, Alfred's father. (Courtesy of
   Jonathan Reeve, JRb39fp671t 800900)
3. The ring of Æthelswith, Alfred's sister. (Courtesy of Jonathan
   Reeve, JRb39fp671tr 800900)
4. The statue of King Alfred in Wantage. (Courtesy of James Platt)
5. A page from the *Anglo-Saxon Chronicle*, thought to have been
   commissioned by Alfred. (Courtesy of Stephen Porter)
6. A depiction of Alfred in a compilation of Anglo-Saxon,

Norman and Angevin law codes. (Courtesy of the British Library, Cotton MS. Claudius D. ii, f. 8.)

7. Photograph of the skulls found by John Mellor in 1866–7 and those excavated from the Unmarked Grave in 2013, demonstrating that they are the same. (Photograph of the five skulls courtesy of Hampshire Archives and Local Studies and photographs of the skulls from the Unmarked Grave courtesy of the University of Winchester)

8. The skulls in the grave. (Courtesy of the University of Winchester)

9. The pelvic bone discovered in 1999, thought to belong to Alfred the Great, or Edward the Elder. (Courtesy of the University of Winchester)

10. Looking into the Unmarked Grave. (Courtesy of the University of Winchester)

11. The bones in the Unmarked Grave prior to excavation. (Courtesy of the University of Winchester)

12. The gravestone slab. (Courtesy of the University of Winchester)

13. Plan of Hyde Abbey as revealed during the building works for the new Bridewell in 1788, with the location of the high altar at 'h' and the three stone coffins at 'a'. (From Howard 1800, courtesy of Katie Tucker)

14. G. F. Watts' *Alfred Inciting the Saxons to Resist the Landing of the Danes*. Alfred is the central figure pointing the sword. (Courtesy of Jonathan Reeve, JRb60p136 800900)

15. A depiction of a Viking ship from near the time of Alfred the Great. The image is from a picture stone in Stenkyrka, Gotland, Sweden. (Courtesy of Jonathan Reeve, JR2231b39fb488 700800)

Bibliography

Abels, Richard (1988). *Lordship and Military Obligation in Anglo-Saxon England*. British Museum Publications (London).

Abels, Richard (1998). *Alfred the Great: War, Kingship and Culture in Anglo-Saxon England*. Routledge (London).

Alexander, Michael (1977). *The Earliest English Poems*. Penguin (Harmondsworth).

Bately, Janet (ed.) (1980). *The Old English Orosius*. Oxford University Press (Oxford).

BBC (2013). 'Richard III Dig: DNA Confirms Bones are King's'. *BBC News*, 4 February 2013. [http://www.bbc.com/news/uk-england-leicestershire-21063882]

Bede (1990). *Ecclesiastical History of the English People*. Penguin (London).

Biddle, M. and Kjølbye-Biddle, B. (1992). 'Repton and the Vikings', in *Antiquity: A Quarterly Review of Archaeology*. Volume 66, Number 250, pp. 36–51. [http://www.archeurope.com/_texts/00008.pdf]

Biddle, M. and Kjølbye-Biddle, B. (2001). 'Repton and the "great heathen army", 873–4', in J. Graham-Campbell, R. Hall, J. Jesch and D. N. Parsons (eds) *Vikings and the Danelaw. Selected Papers from the Proceedings of the Thirteenth Viking Congress*. Oxbow Books (Oxford), pp. 45–96.

Blair, Peter Hunter (1977). *An Introduction to Anglo-Saxon England*. Cambridge University Press (Cambridge).

Boethius (1900). *King Alfred's Version of the Consolations of Boethius*. Translated by Walter Sedgefield. Clarendon Press (Oxford). [http://www.uky.edu/~kiernan/ENG720/SdgTrans/ SedgefieldTranslation.htm]

Bogan, P. (1986). 'Where is King Alfred Buried?', *Winchester Cathedral Record 55*.

Bowker, A. (1902). *The King Alfred Millenary: A Record of the Proceedings of the National Commemoration*. Macmillan (London).

Brooks, Nicholas (1984). *The Early History of the Church of Canterbury*. Leicester University Press (Leicester).

Campbell, James (ed.) (1982). *The Anglo-Saxons*. Phaidon Press (Oxford).

Church Monuments Society. 'Notes and Queries about the Mortuary Chests'. [http://www.churchmonumentssociety.org/Mortuary_ Chests.html]

Colgrave, Bertram (1985). *Felix's Life of Saint Guthlac*. Cambridge University Press (Cambridge).

Collier, C. (1870). 'Report of Committee Appointed to Enquire into the Reputed Discoveries at Hyde', *Proceedings of the Winchester and Hampshire Scientific and Literary Society 1*.

Crawford, Sally (2009). *Daily Life in Anglo-Saxon England*. Greenwood World Publishing (Oxford).

Crook, J. (2000). *The Architectural Setting of the Cult of Saints in the early Christian West.* Oxford University Press (Oxford).

de Gray Birch, W. (ed.) (1892). *Liber Vitae: Register and Martyrology of New Minster and Hyde Abbey, Winchester.* Simpkin and Co. (London).

Dodsworth, R. and Dugdale, G. (1655). *Monasticon Anglicanum Vol. I.* Hodgkinson (London).

Edwards, E. (ed.) (1866). *Liber Monasterii de Hyda.* Longmans (London).

Forester, T. (ed.) (1854). *The Chronicle of Florence of Worcester with the Two Continuations.* Henry Bohn (London).

Gething, Paul and Albert, Edoardo (2012). *Northumbria: The Lost Kingdom.* The History Press (Stroud).

Gibson, E. (1722). *Britannia, or a Chorographical Description of Great Britain and Ireland, Together with the Adjacent Islands. Written in Latin by William Camden and Translated into English, with Additions and Improvements.* Awnsham Churchill (London).

Giles, J. A. (1847). *William of Malmesbury's Chronicle of the Kings of England.* Henry G. Bohn (London).

Grierson, P. (1940). 'Grimbald of St. Bertin's', *English Historical Review* 220.

Hardy, T. D. (1840). *Willelmi Malmesbiriensis Monachi, Gesta Regum Anglorum.* Sumptibus Societatis (London).

Haywood, John (2006). *Dark Age Naval Power: Frankish & Anglo-Saxon Seafaring Activity.* Anglo-Saxon Books (Hockwold-cum-Wilton).

Higham, N. J. (1993). *The Kingdom of Northumbria AD 350–1100.* Alan Sutton (Dover).

Hill, Paul (2012). *The Anglo-Saxons at War 800–1066.* Pen &

Sword Books (Barnsley).

Hindley, Geoffrey (2006). *A Brief History of the Anglo-Saxons*. Constable & Robinson (London).

Horspool, David (2014). *Alfred the Great*. Amberley Publishing (Stroud).

Howard, H. (1800). 'Enquiries Concerning the Tomb of King Alfred, at Hyde Abbey, near Winchester', *Archaeologia* 13 (1800).

Hughes, T. (1901). *Alfred the Great* Macmillan (London).

Ingram, Revd James (trans.) (1912). *The Anglo-Saxon Chronicle*. Everyman Press (London). [http://www.britannia.com/history/docs/asintro2.html]

Kennedy, M. (1999). 'Riddle of Alfred's Bones'. *The Guardian*, 27 October 1999. [http://www.theguardian.com/uk/1999/oct/27/3]

Keynes, Simon and Lapidge, Michael (trans) (2004). *Alfred the Great: Asser's* Life of King Alfred *and Other Contemporary Sources*. Penguin (London).

Lapidge, Michael, Blair, John, Keynes, Simon and Scragg, Donald (eds) (2001). *The Blackwell Encyclopaedia of Anglo-Saxon England*. Blackwell Publishing (Oxford).

Luard, H. R. (ed.) (1865). *Annales Monastici vol. II*. Longmans (London).

Marren, Peter (2006). *Battles of the Dark Ages*. Pen & Sword Books (Barnsley).

Mayr-Harting, Henry (1991). *The Coming of Christianity to Anglo-Saxon England*. B. T. Batsford (London).

Mellor, J. (1871). *The Curious Particulars Related to King Alfred's Death and Burial Never Before Made Public*. James Gibbs (Canterbury).

Moffat, Alistair (2013). *The British: A Genetic Journey*. Birlinn (Edinburgh).

Nelson, Janet L (2004). 'Æthelwulf (*d.* 858)', *Oxford Dictionary of National Biography*. Oxford University Press (Oxford) [http://www.oxforddnb.com/view/article/8921]

Peddie, John (1992). *Alfred the Good Soldier: His Life & Campaigns*. Millstream Books (Bath).

Pollard, Justin (2006). *Alfred the Great: the Man who Made England*. John Murray (London).

Richards, J. D. (2003). 'Pagans and Christians at the Frontier: Viking Burial in the Danelaw', in Carver, M. O. H. (ed.). *The Cross Goes North: Processes of Conversion in Northern Europe, AD 300–1300*. York Medieval Press in association with Boydell & Brewer (York/Woodbridge), pp. 383–395. [http://eprints.whiterose.ac.uk/archive/00000755/]

Robertson, A. J. (1956). *Anglo-Saxon Charters*. Cambridge University Press (Cambridge).

Sawyer, Peter (2013). *The Wealth of Anglo-Saxon England*. Oxford University Press (Oxford).

Scobie, G. S. 'Report on the Excavations at Hyde Abbey, 1995–9'. Winchester Museums Archive: HA 95–99.

Sedgefield, Walter (1900). *King Alfred's Version of the Consolations of Boethius: Done into Modern English*. [http://www.uky.edu/~kiernan/ENG720/SdgTrans/SedgefieldTranslation.htm]

Silverman, R. (2013). 'After Richard III, Archaeologists Set Their Sights on Alfred the Great'. *The Telegraph*, 5 February 2013. [http://www.telegraph.co.uk/science/science-news/9848984/After-Richard-III-archaeologists-set-their-sights-on-Alfred-the-Great.html]

Smith, L. T. (1907). *The Itinerary of John Leland* George Bell (London).

Smyth, Alfred P. (1995). *King Alfred the Great*. Oxford University Press (Oxford).

Southern Daily Echo (2014). 'DNA Tests Begin on Bones of "King Canute"'. *Southern Daily Echo*, 17 April 2014. [http://www.dailyecho.co.uk/heritage/news/11153641.DNA_tests_begin_on_bones_of_King_Canute]

Stevenson, W. H. (ed.) (1904). *Asser's Life of King Alfred, together with the Annals of Saint Neots.* Clarendon Press (Oxford).

Sturdy, David (1995). *Alfred the Great.* Constable (London).

Sweet, Henry (ed.) and Kenneth Cutler (trans.) (1961). 'The Martyrdom of St Edmund, King of East Anglia' in *Anglo-Saxon Primer*. Clarendon Press (Oxford). [http://www.fordham.edu/halsall/source/870abbo-edmund.asp]

Thomas, I. G. (1974). *The Cult of Saints' Relics in Medieval England.* PhD thesis (University of London).

Thorpe, B. (ed.) (1861). *The Anglo-Saxon Chronicle Vol. II: Translation.* Longmans (London).

University of Bristol (2010). 'Bones Confirmed as those of Saxon Princess Eadgyth'. *University of Bristol*, 17 June 2010. [http://www.bris.ac.uk/news/2010/7073.html]

Welch, Martin (1992). *English Heritage Book of Anglo-Saxon England.* B. T. Batsford (London).

Whipple, T. (2013). 'Alfred the Great Next in Line to Be Dug Up', *The Times*, 5 February 2013.

Whitelock, Dorothy (1979). *English Historical Documents; Volume 1, 500–1041.* Eyre & Spottiswode (London).

Wood, Michael (2003). *In Search of the Dark Ages.* BBC Worldwide Ltd (London).

Woodruff, Douglas (1974). *The Life and Times of Alfred the Great.* Weidenfeld and Nicolson (London).

Wright, J. P. (1968). 'Remarkable Skulls', *The Gentleman's Magazine* 225.

Acknowledgements
Dr Katie Tucker

The funding for the excavation of the Unmarked Grave was provided by Hyde900. I would also like to personally thank Rose Burns, Steve Marper, Edward Fennell and Sophie Cunningham Dawe from Hyde900 for their dedication to the project and all the help they have provided me over the last year and a bit.

The funding for the analysis phase of the project was provided by the BBC and I would like to thank Chris Granlund, Nigel Walk, Robin Dashwood, Marianne Bille and Sam Elvin for all their help with the project.

From the University of Winchester, I would like to thank Dr Nick Thorpe, who has headed the project; David Ashby and Adam Fellingham, who very ably assisted me during the excavation; Briony Lalor, for giving up a Saturday to help me wash bones; Dr Simon Roffey, who had been involved with the project from an early stage and suggested to Hyde900 that I would be a suitable person to take it further; Dr Ryan Lavelle and Professor Barbara Yorke, who provided help with the medieval sources; and the senior management team and Press Office.

From the Diocese, I would like to thank the Reverend Cliff Bannister and their Press Officer, Nick Edmonds.

The radiocarbon analysis was carried out by Professor Tom Higham at the Oxford Radiocarbon Accelerator Unit and I would like to thank him for accommodating our complicated and sometimes last-minute requests into his very busy schedule.

Access to the archive for the 1990s excavations at Hyde Abbey was provided by Helen Rees at Winchester Museums Service, Alys Blakeway tracked down documents for me at the Winchester Record Office, and Nathalie Barrett made copies of plans, and I would like to thank them all for making it much easier for me to complete my research.

Index